MEMOIRS OF A WATCH SALESMAN

by

Joseph Aquino

ISBN Paperback: 979-8-9868107-0-6

Library of Congress Number: TXu 2-279-046

Printed in the United States of America

Memoirs of a Watch Salesman

This book is for EVERY salesperson, EVERY real estate broker, and for EVERYDAY people.

> "A NON-FICTION
> THAT READS AS A FICTION"

This book is,

COMPELLING

LOVEABLE

Gripping

HAIR RAISING   SORRY TO SEE IT END

MUST RE-READ

enthralling   UNPUTDOWNABLE

Spellbinding

ENGROSSING

For my wife Suzanne, my rock.

TABLE OF CONTENTS

WHAT'S INSIDE

Read how Joe Aquino got his start in NYC commercial real estate beginning as a table top salesman on the streets of Manhattan. Enjoy his gripping, spellbinding - Tell All - adventures. Laugh, learn and hear his sales, management and NYC real estate escapades starting from the 70's, running to present day! Enjoy this time capsule adventure that is full of inspiration, but without intrigue, lies and betrayal!

ACKNOWLEDGEMENTS

Special thanks to Lisa Keys, a dear friend who worked tirelessly to edit this book. Also, thanks to all my mentors who taught me along the way. I enjoyed writing about our adventures. Finally, thanks to Larry Silverstein and Aby Rosen for sponsoring my company, JA ACRES, into REBNY. Here's to those who wish us well; all the rest can go to Hell!

PREFACE

Everyone's got a story. This is mine — a true rags-to-riches story that starts on the Bicentennial, 1976, on the streets of Manhattan.

I've spent my early life on the streets of New York — selling, hustling, building, and rebuilding. Back then, I was living in a far-from-fancy hotel. A few blocks away was the famous Chelsea Hotel, where Dylan, Joplin, and Hendrix once stayed. My place? A lot rougher. Keith Haring, the legendary artist, and Dee Dee Ramone of The Ramones lived in mine. On that gritty corner of Lexington Avenue and 24th Street, we were surrounded by pimps, prostitutes, and drug dealers. I lived here with a band of hustlers — all of us working for the same outfit, a company selling merchandise on the streets of NYC.

We sold copper-clad pots, knives and glassware sets, and bottles of perfume. I was recruited out in Brooklyn and, overnight, found myself working the busiest corners in Manhattan — right across from Macy's and May's department stores. That's where I learned to bark people cold, win their trust, and close a deal. Jimmy Fallon was discovered as a stand-up comic on a corner in Times Square, me a stand-up salesman in Brooklyn

From there, the company moved on to watches — selling them door-to-door to store owners, not as wholesale stock but as personal pieces, gifts they could give their families or wear themselves. Then came the fitness boom. Nobody worked out back then, but I was running health clubs, learning how to sell memberships on the spot, run a business, and manage a full profit-and-loss operation. The company eventually merged with a larger company, and they were doing a billion dollars in sales nationally. And then I pivoted again — becoming one of New York's top commercial real estate brokers, riding the wave of international retailers flooding into Manhattan and other major U.S. cities, while working alongside some of the most prominent property owners in the world.

My career's been anything but ordinary. I've worked with world-class luxury brands, billion-dollar landlords, and some of the biggest names in fashion, hospitality, and finance. I've also been betrayed, knocked down, written off — but as you'll see in these pages, I always got back up.

This isn't just a memoir about real estate or business. It's about resilience and refusing to give in to failure. About finding joy in the grind. About learning to navigate, to adapt, to find new ways of doing things. About how to forgive — but never forget — and how to keep swinging, no matter how many times life takes a shot at you.

So here it is: my story, in my words. The wins, the losses, the lessons. An old-school and new-school way of doing business — my 50-year journey.

I hope it inspires you to write your own.

— **Joseph Aquino**

Brooklyn born, New York made

I. THE PEDDLING YEARS

October 4th, 1955. The Brooklyn Dodgers win their first World Series in their franchise history when they finally beat the New York Yankees in the seventh game. A baby was born that week near the Dodgers' home stadium, Ebbets Field. A neighbor tells the baby's mother, "Your son was born under winning planets."

In the early 1970s, I dropped out of my first semester of Baruch College. I was seventeen years old. During the semester, I had been selling fragrances on top of a coffee table on Park Avenue South in Manhattan, because I sometimes had three- to-four-hour breaks and I wanted to make use of my time. I had mistakenly marked "part-time" on my registration form, and that's why I had a staggered school schedule. It was the first year that Baruch used computers to schedule the students and there was no chance to change the timing. I was the first one in my family to go to college. I was clueless as to the procedure and I missed the deadline to make changes.

I had found a wholesaler who was the boyfriend of my mom's best girlfriend, and I used my income tax refund check to buy products. The store was located on East 17th Street, between Union Square and Fifth Avenue. The wholesalers were lined up back-to-back on the street. All you saw were carts with merchandise being whisked back and forth from the store to waiting vehicles by the curb. After my introduction to Fred, the owner, I was introduced to the world of items that could be peddled on the streets of New York City. Shortly into my visit, fragrances caught my eye. There was a large stock of Charlie perfume, which was the most popular brand in the marketplace, with huge TV ad support. Along with Charlie, I also had an opportunity to sell a Nina Ricci perfume, L' Air du Temps, which was equally famous. What attracted me to the Nina Ricci was the plastic dove with open wings that sat on top of the bottle. I could purchase bottles of perfume for one dollar and sell them for three. On my first day, I sold out fast. This kept me busy on my long breaks.

I realized that Baruch wasn't for me, for I found that when I was not selling fragrances, I was gaping at the pretty girls coming out of Visual Arts school, one block down. Even though I got an A- in art, I did not want to start an art career. I did not feel that that was the way to earn a stable income.

After I left school and prior to Mother's Day, a friend of mine and I went to a nursery to buy plants to sell to husbands and children. We set out to sell them on Flatbush Avenue by the Kings Plaza shopping mall. Not yet being retail-savvy, I convinced my colleague to buy smaller plants because they were less expensive. And at the end of the day, we only sold one.

My friend said, "I knew we made a mistake, because no one brings small plants home to Mom on Mother's Day."

It was a good lesson, one I never forgot: Don't be cheap when you want big things to happen.

A month after Mother's Day, I went back to my friend Fred the wholesaler and asked him if he had any larger-tag items besides perfume. He happily showed me a variety of knife sets which were reasonable in price. I saw an opportunity to make a nice mark-up selling them on the street, so I bought a variety.

On my first outing, in Brooklyn by the junction on the corner of Flatbush Avenue and Avenue H, I did nicely selling sets by always having cash in hand, giving customers their correct change. A junkie approached the table. I knew he was not looking to buy any of my knives. He was looking at the cash.

I put the money in my pocket and grasped the handle of a huge 14-inch steak knife. The drugged man immediately took a step back. As soon as this happened, out of nowhere, two fellows approached my table and started talking to me as though they knew me. At that point, the junkie saw he was outnumbered, and he fled. I thanked the two fellows, whose names I learned were Peter and Ronnie. Peter was a stubby white fellow who sweated profusely, and Ronnie was a suave African American gent sporting a thin Errol Flynn mustache with Jheri-curled hair.

Peter started smooth-talking me with the idea that I might work for them. They had a peddling operation in Manhattan with twenty guys and they sold a variety of kitchen products. They wanted me to see the operation the following day, a Saturday. I backed off thinking it was a scam. Companies like that would get you to invest in their product that usually did not sell, and you got stuck laying out a lot of money for useless stuff. I told Peter, "I have no money to invest."

Peter laughed and said, "We don't want your money, we want you." He followed that remark by saying that they had been watching me in the car for some time and that I was a great salesman, selling products to everyone who approached my table. I still had my guard up, but I was flattered.

I finally said, "I can't make it tomorrow, I'll come by Monday morning."

Peter insisted, "No, it has to be tomorrow."

The following day, I arrived at 8:00 A.M. Peter and Ronnie were located in Manhattan's "Fur District," on West 30th Street between Sixth and Seventh Avenues. They were working out of a storefront, and it looked pretty safe. It was like Fred's place, but the adjacent stores were furriers, not wholesale merchandisers. They were situated across from the 14th Precinct police station. And sure enough they had twenty people hustling products onto vans from the backs of the stores. The energy felt good. Everyone was hustling, smiling, and joking. I immediately got a good vibe. I knew I could do this.

Every team had a standing trolley car. After a van was filled with goods, three guys, including me, would jump into the back. The driver would set us up on busy corners in Manhattan. These included 14th Street on Union Square across from Macy's Department store and Sixth Avenue and 35th Street across from Macy's flagship store.

The driver dropped the goods on the corner and when he left, I counted that I had a total of twenty -six boxes which included ten boxes of assorted tumblers, drinking glasses, and wine glasses, along with four copper-clad pots sets and ten boxes that included forty-three-piece Sheffield knife sets, were made in England, that even included an apple corer. And let's not forget the crock-pots. I had two of those as well.

The last word the driver told me was that the first item someone touches is usually what they eventually buy.

Almost immediately, a flock of women and a few men surrounded me. I was working with three to four people at a time, noticing who was touching what first: the key give-away as to what they really wanted. Before I knew it, goods were tied up with packing strings along with those handy wood handles, money was exchanged, and the products were taken away by people with happy faces, convinced that they had gotten a good deal. Shortly thereafter, my pile of goods that started at three feet tall by six feet wide was reduced to the ground that I was standing on. I sold out in two hours.

The driver had told me that he would be back by five o'clock to pick me up. It was only one o'clock, so I decided to head back to the store with the cart and cash in my pocket.

When I entered the store, Peter said, "What happened? Are you okay? Did the cops stop you? And where is the merchandise?"

I pulled out a roll of cash three inches thick. Peter smiled and I smiled back. He said, "I knew you had it in you. I told Ronnie; I knew you were going to be great." He patted me on the back, and he walked me over to Ronnie. He said, "Joey sold out in two hours."

Ronnie always smoked Nat Sherman cigarettes. He had a deep voice, a baritone for sure. He shook my hand, and said, "Congrats, Joey and welcome aboard."

Peter was short and stubby like the comedian Lou Costello or (for the newer generation who don't know Costello) John Belushi. He had long greasy hair and always looked like he needed a shower. He was constantly sweating. Nevertheless, he was personable. I liked him from the get-go, and I have never forgotten the day he recruited me off the streets of Brooklyn.

That summer was going great. I was running my own crew—three men and myself—practically selling out every day. I realized that I had talent, because the other fellows didn't get the sales I did and were always returning goods.

Right before the Bicentennial (1976), Peter leased a brand-new Ford EconoVan that I brought home to Mom—full of merchandise. Mom immediately thought I was involved with the mob, but I assured her we were legit. However, later, I learned that Peter was handing out false identification cards to the workers who were getting daily fines. I never received a ticket from a police officer, maybe because I was never on the corner that long.

It was August, and we were seeing temperatures in the nineties. I got one of my bronchial colds and one morning I called in sick.

Peter heard it in my voice and said, "Stay home, we will be fine." On that day, the police from the 14th Precinct, across the street, stormed the store and locked up Peter and Ronnie and threw them into the clink for the night.

Ronnie immediately thought I had squealed because I had not shown up for work that day. I told Peter that I couldn't have done that because I didn't know that he was handing out false I.D. cards. Peter never doubted me.

I found out that Peter was a former heroin addict and that now he was on the city run methadone program, taking daily doses of methadone during the week and a hefty double dose on the weekends.

I never let the drugs get between Peter and me. I never had the desire to do them. I never touched them. I knew if I did them once, I would be finished. I knew from Peter that drugs cannot be your friends. They take you down instantly.

I respected Peter, because he was teaching me, as he would call it, "The Science of Selling." He was a master salesman, having risen from the ranks of door-to-door encyclopedia and subscription magazine salesman. Now, because of his condition, he had become a hustler, using the same sales methods as he did for selling the books and subscriptions. Peter was old-school. He did not sell the steak; he sold the sizzle. Another lesson learned.

Peter announced the day he was let out of jail that he never wanted to go back. He was claustrophobic, and that night took a few years off his life.

Peter announced the same day via phone that the peddling operation was finished. He told me he was going to convert to a door-to-door operation. I immediately thought, "How the heck are we going to carry the goods?" I expressed that thought to Peter. He said, "Joey, we are not."

"Ok, then what are we going to sell?"

"I do not know yet, but I am going to go into the market this week to find a product."

Peter told me to take the rest of the week off, which was fine with me since I was still getting over my cold. About a week went by before I got a call from Peter to come in the next day: he found a product. I was feeling much better the following day, when I arrived at 10:00.

Peter handed me a blue watch box in a white sleeve. I opened it and read the dial: Kronotron. The watch had a sunny iridescent dial with three pushers, and each pusher had its own knob on the right side of the case. The watch had weight and I recognized the skin diver's dial on the bottom, followed by the middle crown for the time and date. The top dial gives you the different times of major cities around the world. All you had to do was put New York City in the present time and you could see what the time was in New Delhi or Zurich.

I was immediately impressed. Peter asked, "Do you think you can sell them?"

"Sure, what's next.'

"I have already been out with them for a couple of days and today I am going to show you how to sell them."

Sure enough, I got to see the master selling. It appeared Peter was handing these watches out like gumdrops. Nobody said no to him, and in two hours, Peter had sold out. I was picking up Peter's sales techniques—some of which I never knew existed. This was the first of many days of watching and listening to Peter on how to sell this product effectively.

"Are you ready to take a try at this tomorrow?" he asked. I immediately said; "Yeah, sure!"

The following day, I was handed a brown small corrugated box with 10 watches inside. With them, I hit as many Midtown stores as I could, going into all the side street and main avenue stores. We never knocked on residential doors: we only peddled to stores, or pitched people on the street if they were busy loading a truck or van. The watches were sold as personal items or gifts, never as a wholesale item.

The first day, I didn't use any of the techniques that Peter taught me, because they were so new, but somehow, I managed to sell eight of the ten watches.

Over the next few weeks, we started to ramp up the new operation. Not all the peddlers converted, because selling door-to-door took much more savvy than peddling on the street corner. Robert and Ed stayed on, and the rest fell by the wayside. Peter started running ads, and soon we had six and seven more people. Peter would tell me we would never have a group of twenty anymore, and that the company would be a much smaller and tighter group. By now, I had been introduced to Barry, whose mom was a star sales lady selling Yellow Page ads. Barry was a chip off the old block, and he would take us out to a different territory every day. We would hit all the high streets in all five boroughs and Long Island too. Some of our favorite streets outside of Manhattan were 86th Street and Coney Island Avenue in Brooklyn, Austin Street or Queens Boulevard in Queens, and the main streets of Manhasset and Huntington on Long Island.

Finally, I started coming into my own selling watches consistently. Peter taught that sometimes you would sell out in an hour and other days it could take five to six hours. Either way, you would hit every store you came to and never stop. Peter would say, "Never pass one, because you never know where the sale will come from!" He also would say, "Hit the ones that look like they won't buy, because those are the virgins that everyone else passes." Sure enough, if I saw unruly people, I would feel excited. I would pitch them and always get the sale. He also advised me, "Never stay with negative customers." Just thank them and move on. All valuable lessons.

By now, Peter had a canned presentation that taught me and the other salespersons how to answer objections. In the science of selling, no matter what product or service you are selling, there are always the same 10 objections not to buy. So, it's simple: If you master these objections, your chances of selling will increase ten-fold.

Here is a little of what Peter taught us: you would walk into the store and about five feet from the counter you would stop, look up and nod. You would wait for the nod back. Peter would explain that this area was the customer's safe zone, and you would basically be asking permission to enter it.

Then you would either say that Bob at the deli had just got one and he thought you would like one too. And then you would stay silent waiting for the response: invariably, "One of what?" Or you could just go into your pitch: "We just had a gift show at the Coliseum in New York—and instead of shipping them back and giving them back, we were in the area, and we thought you would want one."

Then we would pause and wait for the other person to say, "Want one what?"

I would smile and stumble a little as I pulled out the blue box in the white sleeve, like this was new to me. I would say, "These are the Kronotron - chronographs, you know, like Seiko." I would never say they were Seiko, which was a large-selling watch of this period. I would follow up by saying, "It's a three function skin divers watch that tells the time of all the different cities around the world." I would immediately go into the presentation, aligning New York to the present time showing them how they could see all the different times of all the other cities around the world. I would demonstrate the skin divers dial and how it turns, and then I would open the pusher to the time and date and show how the arms to the watch moved. Right after the features I would go into the price by saying the manufacturer's suggested retail price is $125, and point to the tag. Then I would say, "But that's the manufacturer's retail price, they really go for about $60 to $65 dollars in the stores. Today we are selling them for $30 apiece." I would pause and say, "They are nice, right?" and wait for an answer.

At this point, the customers would have the watch in their hands or on their wrist, putting the watch up to their ear listening to the ticking. Then you would pre qualify them by saying things like "If you would get this, would you buy it for yourself or a friend?" After they answered, they would always have a few questions or objections that I would answer. We were taught once you answer an objection, then proceed to close. I would show them the two-year warranty it came with, from the Geneva Watch company on West 39th Street and tell them to make a copy for themselves, because you only get one copy.

Then it was time to close the sale. Here is how I did it: Negotiating the price was one way to close. For example, if you came down too quickly, they always took you lower. So, you always had to give them a little tug of war. Finally, they might say, I'll give you $20, take it or leave it. Peter taught us not to say yes. Instead, I was taught to reply, "Is that cash?" ...and that always got a laugh. The customer would always say something like, "What do you think, I was going to give you a check?"

Then, I would finish the sale by saying "Okay, you win!" looking beat, as if they had won the battle.

The deal was concluded. Another way to close after providing the price and answering their objections, "Ok, you see how you only have one copy of the warranty?" I would wait for a nod. I would say, "Don't make this mistake, make a copy! (nodding my head up and down) Because you don't want to send it in and you forgot where you sent it too. " I would pause. Then follow up by saying; " Because you want a copy for your records, right?" They would nod, and then I would close the case of the watch, with the watch inside, and say, "I would appreciate it if you would give me small bills, I have been getting big bills all day." I would shut up. Peter taught us, the first person who talks, loses. At this point of the sale, they were either sold, or you would have to address another objection.

Lesson learned: Have a saleable product, give a good presentation, and close in a timely manner.

Barry was a great leader. He would always pick good territories and we would go out two hours in the morning and meet back in a diner. We would all have lunch together and then we would go out for another two hours and meet back at about four o'clock. We would all take the subway or the train back to the office.

One day Peter announced a contest. The highest number of sales would get $100. That was a lot of money back then. During this period, we had three divisions in the marketplace, and everyone got 12 watches each. That morning I sold out by lunch and said I just won $100 to Barry. Donald, one of the other salespeople on my team, got stopped by the police and was told if he was caught selling in town again—we were in Manhasset—he would spend the night in jail. So, Barry took his 12 pieces and gave them to me. Admittedly, I was a little peeved. I resisted, but he said, "Look at it this way: you are on a roll. No one in the company has ever sold twenty-four pieces—including me—in one day, so go for it!"

On my second pitch that afternoon, I got lucky, I sold all 12 pieces to the service department of a car dealership. It was December leading up to Christmas and the manager said, "If you give me a good deal, I'll take them all off your hands."

"Of course,' I said. "Is it cash?" He laughed, and then I said, "Okay, "and I sold the watches to him at my trade-in price. I didn't make money on the sale, but I didn't lose money and I knew then that I had won the $100.

When I returned to the office, I put a sad face on. I was a little manic back then and people knew if I had had a bad day. Robert knew he had me. I said to him, "How did you do?" He turned his box upside down and nothing came out, showing me he sold out his 12 pieces.

"How did you do?"

I turned two boxes upside down and shook them. He said, "I don't understand."

I explained, "Donald got picked up by the police so Barry gave me his 12 pieces and I sold them too. I sold twenty-four watches in total."

Robert was upset to say the least. Peter gave me a big handshake in front of everyone and gave me a crisp $100 bill. Nobody had ever sold these many watches in one day. Lesson learned, The harder you work, the luckier you get!

By now, I had moved into the George Washington Hotel. I had to, for I was too exhausted, taking mass transit to and from the territories and then another two hours back and forth to Brooklyn. It was too much. Mom understood. My sister was already out of the house and now it was my turn. However, I enjoyed coming home every weekend to be with my friends and getting home cooked meals, especially on Sunday when mom always cooked an Italian dish of pasta with meatballs.

Hotel George Washington had a variety of people living in it: mostly senior citizens on a fixed income. The rent was $50 a week, and every week we lined up at the desk to pay our bill in cash.

Outside of the hotel, no matter what time of day, there were always prostitutes looking to turn a trick. At nighttime, the number tripled. People from all over used to drive into this area to meet and greet my neighbors. Among the prostitutes there was an occasional pimp roaming around along with the local drug dealers. Somehow, we all lived happily together in this microcosm of Manhattan. Let us not forget my alma mater, Baruch College, was right across the street and the College Bookstore on the other corner of Lexington Avenue and 23rd Street was the first store that Leonard Riggio, the founder of Barnes & Noble bookstore cut his teeth in the book business selling and trading books for resale to and from the college students. During this period, Rock Stars like Patty Smith, Jimmy Hendrix, and Bob Dylan were staying or visiting The Chelsea Hotel that was several blocks away, along with the famed Max's Kansas City that was a bar and music venue where artists like David Bowie, Lou Reed and The Velvet Underground played frequently. At my hotel Keith Haring was a student at Visual Arts down the block and had a cheap apartment along with Dee Dee Ramone from the famous punk rock band, The Ramones. New York City was at its grittiest stage with great music being produced daily. Glam Rock was at its peak with bands like Kiss and Bowie wearing what appeared to be women's make-up on stage. On Friday afternoons, Scott Muni, a disc jockey from radio station, WNEW would play new hits from London every Friday afternoon from 3 to 6 pm and this went on for years. Central Park during the summer was playing great concerts with such groups or single musicians as Mountain, Richie Havens, Jefferson Starship, Procol Harum, Mandril, and Sha Na Na and tickets were $2.50 per person. You could see concerts at the ice skating rink that was converted into a concert venue during the summer. Schaefer Beer was the host there, or you could see a free concert at The Naumburg BandShell that was nearby in the park.

Peter worked out a deal with the General Manager of the George Washington Hotel, and we got to use the 10,000-square-foot mezzanine for our morning sales meetings. We would also meet there on our return later in the day. Peter at first ran the meetings, but eventually I took over that task. I enjoyed motivating the troops in the morning right before we went out onto the market.

Peter had a special way of hiring new salespeople. He would put an ad in the newspaper for a stock person. This job didn't exist. He would interview everyone. Sometimes up to fifty people would show up. He would chat with them and tell them that the position was filled. But, if he felt that a person had sales ability, he would say something to the effect that there was another position available. He would describe it and the pay scale, and see if they would bite. He would always find the best talent. Then it was my job to take them out for three days and show them how easy it was to sell the product. After training, he would convert them from salary to commission. He was able to do this because I made the job seem so effortless. Furthermore, the stock job paid $90—which meant that after taxes, in those days, maybe the take-home came to $60.

He would tell them about his Maximum Incentive Program, and he would show them how much commission one could make selling the product. Every time, they would convert. By selling watches, back in the 1970s, a salesman could easily make $250 or more a week, which was a lot of money.

On Friday nights, before going home, sometimes Tony and I used to go up to Peter's hotel room to give him the receivables. At this point Peter has already taken his double dose of methadone. We would give him the money and he would start to count it while he was rocking forwards and backwards on his chair. This wasn't every Friday, but we did see this often. Tony and I used to laugh—not loudly, because we liked and respected Peter so much—but we used to bet that he was going to fall forward on his face. Sure enough, there would be times when he was at a thirty-degree angle from the floor ready to do a face-plant—then he would just stop and rock himself back into the chair.

Tony was a great guy. Eventually, Tony left and went into a management program to run supermarkets. Today, I believe, he owns and operates three of them

Two years had passed since I was recruited by Peter on the corner of Flatbush Avenue. When you are young, two years can seem like a lifetime. By then, I had walked into every store in the five boroughs and Long Island at least three full times. I was burnt out and the job was not challenging to me anymore.

Another valuable lesson: you need to know when to leave. I was ready for a new chapter in my life. I called Mom and I told her I was coming home. She was delighted. My sister had recently returned home too, having separated from her boyfriend. It was going to be like old times, living with my two favorite women again.

II. THE HEALTH CLUB YEARS

Now I was back at Mom's house, where I grew up, trying to figure out my next move. Many people offered me jobs over the past two years, but I was so loyal to Peter, I never took advantage of any of them. I remembered one time being pitched by the manager of the Jack LaLanne Health Club on Flatbush Avenue in Brooklyn. I decided to give them a try. I was sent to see Eileen Collins at the Biltmore Hotel in Manhattan on Madison Avenue and 43rd Street. She handled all the new hires. The following week I found myself sitting in front of an exceptionally pretty woman. I learned that she had competed as a Miss America contestant. She was the ultimate model of health and beauty. She had beautiful blond hair, light blue eyes, and an award-winning smile, and lots of charm.

I got the job, but before I was assigned to one of the clubs, I had to go through training. The General Manager of the entire operation was a man named Barry Flickstein. He would always start the three-day sales seminar meeting by saying, "What is the number one thing you need to succeed?" The sales trainees would raise their hands and give him answers that he wasn't looking for.

Finally, I raised my hand and said, "Desire."

His face went emotionless, and he said, "That's the right answer, but in all my years of doing this, no one has ever answered it correctly."

The following week, I got assigned to the Kings Highway branch located on Coney Island Avenue, across the street from the Lowes Theatre in Brooklyn. Hank Rosenblum was my manager. We are still great friends today.

The members were mostly older Jewish people who were also members of the Brighton Beach Baths, located not far from the Coney Island amusement park, known for the Cyclone Roller Coaster and other amusement rides.

They loved Jack La Lanne, because it had a full spa, with pool, whirlpool, steam, sauna, and showers. That was besides a full gym with equipment and exercise classes.

Hank immediately took to me and had me working in the gym, escorting customers around the machines, besides training me to be a salesman. He wanted me to get in shape and he started taking me for runs nearby on Ocean Parkway. I started working out on a regular basis. I was still a smoker, but eventually I quit.

The company would have quarterly membership sales drives for new membership, and we would post signs all around the facility announcing the sale. We had sales drives called; Two For One, Summer Free and Winter Free. The signs we posted were about three feet wide and four feet in height and when the sale was coming to an end, we would have a "close out," where we put countdown banner signs over the for-sale signs on all the mirrors, posters, and on the front door facing the street. On the first day of the countdown, the banners would read "10 Days Left," then the next day it would say "9 Days Left," and so on. We would make it an impending event. Then of course, on the last day we had a sign that read: "Last Day." We would do as many sales numbers in that one day as we would regularly do in a whole month.

In the weeks leading to the countdown, Hank would give me the sheets with the names and the phone numbers of all the people who had visited the club for the past six months and he would close my office door and say, "Now, Joey, you are going to call all these people. You are going to be dialing for dollars," and I did.

Sure enough, on the first sales week, I brought about twenty people back to the club to sign up who would never have come back if not for my call and pitch.

We used to give out a lot of promotional items to make the sale. Members could get tights, gym bags, sweatshirts for themselves, and one-month passes for a guest. Hank warned me some of the old-time customers were *schnorrers*. I asked what that meant, and he said, "It's a Yiddish word for a person who is super cheap and is never satisfied when buying. They always want more and more." He told me if there was ever a member that asked for too much, I was to call him a *schnorrer*.

It was the peak of the summer and Mr. and Mrs. Cohen came into my office to reinstate their membership. They were members of the Brighton Beach Baths and the fall season was around the corner when it closed. They were usually older - retired people that wanted to keep *schvitzing*, another Yiddish word which means to sweat while taking a sauna or a steam bath. Brighton Beach Baths had a full spa facility at which they could *schvitz* in the summer and they wanted to do the same during the off-season.

I was certain that this was going to be a quick reinstatement—till Mr. Cohen started negotiating. He started by getting two sets of tights, one for his wife and one for his daughter, then two gym bags, then two sweatshirts, then four one-month passes for friends and family, and then an additional six months on each of their one-year reinstatements. Finally, out of nowhere, with the agreements filled out, Mr. Cohen stood up and said, "Okay, Joey, I have to think about it."

By this time, we were 60 minutes into the meeting. It was then that I fully understood the true meaning of the word *schnorrer*. Mr. Cohen had negotiated each individual item one by one like a surgeon taking out my kidney stones. I let him have it. In a high-pitched voice I said,

"Mr. Cohen, you're a *schnorrer*!"

Suddenly I thought I was standing in front of Mount Vesuvius. Mr. Cohen started screaming at the top of his lungs, "How dare you call me a *schnorrer*!" Hank, whose office was directly next to mine, came in immediately.

He recognized Mr. Cohen and said, "Mr. Cohen, what happened?"

Mr. Cohen said, "Joey called me a *schnorrer*."

Hank was smooth. I think everyone in the facility heard Mr. Cohen scream. Hank laughed and said, "Relax, Mr. Cohen, the joke is on Joey." Mr. Cohen did not understand. Hank followed by saying, "We told Joey if someone was a good negotiator to compliment them and call them a *schnorrer*."

Immediately, Mr. Cohen put his hand on my shoulder and looked me straight in the eye and said, "Joey, never say that word to anyone again. It's a terrible word." Hank and I winked at each other and he stayed a little long to persuade Mr. and Mrs. Cohen to join that day.

What Hank did there was what we call a T.O., which stands for turn-over: another salesman comes into the office with a new point of view and takes over the sale to close the transaction. Phew, close call! Lesson of the day: know when to drop the bomb and then duck.

Shortly thereafter, Jack La Lanne's annual black-tie event took place at the Pierre Hotel—an ultra-luxe property located on Fifth Avenue at 61st Street, across from Central Park. Jack La Lanne always had first class events and they had secured the Grand Ballroom which was designed in the style of the *French Belle Epoque*.

I remember it as though it were yesterday. I was wearing my first rented tuxedo, with suspenders, patent leather shoes, and all the trimmings. I had taken off my jacket and was walking around with my bright white tuxedo shirt with ruffles. There was a staircase that separated the ballroom from one level to the next. I was standing at the top of the stairs and below a man looked up at me. He was Harry Schwartz, the owner of Jack La Lanne. This was our first meeting. Harry did not turn out to be as kind as Peter, my old boss. Peter sold the knives to cut the core out of the apple, Harry was the knife that cut your guts out as though it was the apple core.

Harry's first words to me were, "Where is your jacket?"

At that point, I didn't know who this man was, and how dare he talk to this young cocky twenty-three-year-old Italian-American boy from Brooklyn who had successfully canvassed his heart out for the past two years in the Greater New York area selling watches? I realized he was someone powerful, but didn't know how much power he had. I found out only too soon that he was my new *capo di capo*.

"It's on my chair."

"Go put it on."

Shortly thereafter it was confirmed that he was the big boss when he kicked off the evening meal with a speech to the audience. He was brilliant. He told everyone how he still ate tuna out of a can, because it reminded him when he had no money. His story was no different than that of many successful people who started with nothing.

Hank had told me that Harry had wanted to be an actor and had lived in Hollywood. He had appeared as an extra in Mae West 's movies. He would be the guy with the muscles by the pool. He used to crash all the Hollywood parties just like every other aspiring actor. One day he overheard some woman refer to him as a bum. He never forgot. He said it was amazing, what an experience like that will do to somebody. It turned the direction of his career overnight.

Now that I had officially been baptized by fire, I was enjoying the rhythm of learning to operate a health club. I was quickly taught to wear many hats. On one hand, you had to be a great salesman—as though you were selling Fuller Brushes—while on the other, you had to be a great manager like Ray Kroc at McDonalds. It wasn't enough to bring the income in. You had to keep a clean place and give good service, so that the members would be happy, of course return to use the facilities, and bring in their friends and family.

By the summer of that year, Mom had had her first heart attack, and I was going to the hospital on my days off. By September she had passed away. Mom had been told she had to stay off the salt and my sister told me one night she just broke out the saltshaker and showered her baked potato.

During this period, my mandated hours were from 10 in the morning to 10 at night, four weekdays, and nine to six on Saturdays. Those long hours saved my mental state. I had lost my father when I was 12, and now I had lost Mom in my early twenties. Jack La Lanne became my new family and since I was in a management program, I was working sixty mandated hours a week. My starting position was Program Director. The commute added another 15 hours a week.

For the generation that doesn't know who Jack La Lanne was, he was the first fitness guru that had his own TV show on network television. The show peaked in the 1950s and 60s, but Wikipedia says it went on way into the 80s. La Lanne had two white German shepherds called Happy and Walter that used to appear at the beginning of the show and he used to do calisthenics wearing a jumpsuit with a two-inch spandex belt around his waist. He used a chair to hold on, just like the way a ballet dancer would hold on to the dancing barre. For thirty minutes he would lead a TV audience of mostly women—each presumably with her chair next to her— in a series of exercises. This was back in the day when most women stayed home while the men went to work. The women loved him. Then he used to do different stunts on his birthday, like towing ninety or so boats at a time while he was swimming in a lake.

Harry gave Jack a small royalty for the privilege of using his name. He said at one of our meetings, "I could have built the company without him, but I know every time I pitched someone about health and fitness and mentioned Jack's name, they always got a sparkle in their eye and had a picture in the back of their mind of Jack professing health and fitness on TV."

Remember, this was an early time in the fitness movement, where people didn't work out two to three times a week. Madison Avenue hadn't made such a regimen fashionable yet. Women had questions about building muscle and what happened if they stopped. There was a lot of uncertainty, and the program directors at Jack La Lanne were like priests professing a new gospel of working out on a regular basis. Only bodybuilders worked out regularly and most people didn't want a bodybuilders' physique. So besides selling them on the program, we had to educate them on health and fitness. For example, did you know that every pound of excess fat requires one mile of extra blood vessels? Imparting facts like that was part of promoting health and fitness.

Soon, I was ready to become an assistant manager. That post was responsible for setting up the weekend sales, besides helping the manager with the sales during the week. My manager at Bensonhurst was Norman Kluge and we are still great friends to this day. I compare my health club cronies to military friends: you have them forever.

For the next few years, I was an assistant manager at a few clubs. Besides Bensonhurst, I assisted at City Hall, when Mayor Ed Koch was a member. He used to visit the club in the morning to work out.

One time during a subway strike, I had to stay overnight for a few days because the trains weren't running. That health club was situated in the basement of the Woolworth Building at 233 Broadway, next to the famous Harry's Restaurant.

One night my manager, Rick Gottfried, was reading *The Daily News*. He still had his work clothes on which was a dark blue tracksuit with the company's logo on the jacket and pants. While he was standing, reading, in the middle of the lobby, a mouse ran across the room and went up one of the legs of his pants. Suddenly, he starts hitting his crotch with the newspaper. He continued hitting himself for a good thirty to sixty seconds. There were three other people in the reception area and we all started laughing. Finally, the mouse fell from his pants leg and ran back to the hole in the wall where it came from.

The Vice President promoted me to Manager at the Bensonhurst location, where I had previously worked as an assistant. Back then, every office had voice surveillance boxes for training purposes—now, of course, they're illegal.

We used those machines to monitor how our Program Directors presented our services. One afternoon, I was reviewing a recording of a Program Director qualifying a potential customer. They were walking the prospect through our exercise program, highlighting the equipment, amenities, and outlining the structure of our memberships. We trained them to explain the two-part, one-year plan: the first six months focused on reducing fat and tightening muscle, while the second six months—the maintenance phase—was just as important for keeping the weight off.

We also taught our Program Directors to ask targeted questions like, "How long have you been thinking about getting into shape?" This gave us insight into how long they'd been procrastinating—a key obstacle to achieving fitness goals. Sometimes, our Directors would take a lighter approach, saying something like, "You don't know anyone who procrastinates like that, do you?" Nine times out of ten, the prospect would smile and reply, "Yes—me!"

Once we had that rapport, we'd go over the plan and recommend a one-year membership—six months to see results and six to maintain them. Then we'd review pricing and payment options.

We worked off a four-page interview sheet that covered everything. Once all the commitments were noted, we'd slide the enrollment card across the desk, place a pen next to it, and say, "Okay, Mrs. Jones, fill out the card and get yourself started." Then—silence. We trained our staff not to speak after that, because oddly enough, as I mentioned earlier in the book, the first person to talk usually lost the sale.

This Program Director was doing everything perfectly and at the end it was as though his plane was coming in for a landing. The only problem was, he forgot the part about telling the client to fill out the card. So, the airplane would lift from the runway at that critical point and start to circle the airport again. He missed the landing three more times and finally on the fourth attempt, I knew if I didn't do something, Mrs. Jones was going to say "thank you" and leave.

On the next attempt, just when the plane was going to touch down on the runway, I pressed the button to the intercom in my office and said, "Fill out the card and get yourself started."

Suddenly there was total silence. I thought, "Holy crap, I cannot believe I just did that." I imagined that the lady had run out of the club and the six o'clock nightly news would be arriving soon at my door to do a story on what happened. I immediately went outside to see if I could catch the lady to apologize but saw no one. After walking down the block on both sides, I came back into the club, and I pulled the curtain to the office aside slightly to see what was going on. The lady was filling out the contract. I could not believe I had closed her from the next office.

After she left the building, I asked the salesman what had happened once she heard me. He said, "I just put the card in front of her and she started to fill it out."

Another time, while I was managing Bensonhurst, Anthony, my program director, came into my office with a military-size duffle bag filled with wrapped ounces of marijuana. He told me that two Jamaican fellows will be coming by later to pick up the bag and when I saw them in his office, I should know they are not here for membership.

I said sure, but I realized what he was getting me into. Before the rush, at about 5:30, I saw the two in his office and they're walking out with the bag. They looked like members since they were dressed to work out. Then, suddenly, Anthony opens my office door and throws bundles of cash with rubber bands around them onto my desk and tells me to count them.

He walked out of my office and I said to myself, "I am not touching this money." I didn't flip out, but I approached Tony in his office and told him to take the money back.

That night I told my Vice President about the incident and the following day, Tony got transferred to Kings Highway. I eventually got a call from him, and he called me a rat. I didn't answer back. At that point, he was no longer my problem. Lesson learned: manage your staff and know right from wrong.

Harry started negotiations with Don Wildman from Health and Tennis Corporation of America, located in Chicago, to join his company. Harry and Don came out of Vic Tanny. Vic was the first to have a national gym business. Harry and Don had been vice presidents there. When Vic started selling lifetime memberships, Harry and Don along with the other vice presidents warned Vic that he risked losing his back-end income from the renewals. Vic didn't listen to them—and soon after, the company went bankrupt. Vic had about seven vice presidents, and once Vic closed his operation, all of them went back to their respective towns and started to build their own health club chains.

Don Wildman, who had seen action during the Korean War, was fearless. When he returned to the United States, the first thing he did was get on his knees and kiss the runway at O'Hare Airport in Chicago. Don did the "Ironman" challenge each year in Hawaii. Every year he finished in the number two position for his age group. At that time, he owned and was also running 300 health clubs. The man who beat him each year had fully retired and all he did was train for this event.

Over the years, Don persuaded all the former vice presidents to join Health and Tennis Corporation of America and now it was time to bring Harry on board. It took some time to sell Harry, but eventually, he saw the benefits and we became part of Health and Tennis Corp.

Our brand name was still going to be Jack La Lanne Health Spa

This happened in the early 1980s and within four years we saw incredible growth. We went from sixteen to forty locations practically overnight and these were not small locations. They were huge.

When I was at the Flatbush Avenue branch during this period, the company announced a new contest for us. It was called Operation Upgrade and it was a contest to give the club a cosmetic uplift. We were allowed to use petty cash to buy paint and other items to polish up the club. Immediately, I resolved to do a little work every day, knowing that my competition would wait till the days of the last week. The last few days of the contest I wanted to be finished and focus on getting good sales numbers and I did. I knew my fellow managers would come in with poor sales numbers, because they would be focusing on painting and cleaning.

I motivated the staff to work. We painted all the lockers and walls and stenciled sports figures above the mirrors in the exercise rooms. Karen Shapiro, my assistant, was a commercial artist. She made the templates for the figures, and she sprayed the stencils. We also polished the terrazzo floors in the lobby. We were on schedule till the week prior to inspection, when a torrential rainstorm opened the ceiling and tar fell through the roof and landed all over the rug in the exercise room. I notified John Wilton, with whom I am still friends today, and he managed to have a brand-new carpet delivered and installed for the entire gym prior to the executives' arrival for inspection.

The place looked stunning. Flatbush had been one of the first clubs of the chain and it needed a facelift. When the inspectors (who were gym owners from the other States) arrived, along with Harry Schwartz, they must have been impressed, for I won $500 and dedicated the money to a party for the staff. Harry rarely gives compliments, but he even chimed in, "I can't believe this is Flatbush."

Lesson learned: plan your attack and don't wait for the last minute.

I got assigned to Little Neck in Queens, an affluent working-class community. The club was about 30,000 square feet on two levels. Harry Schwartz frequented the club since he had his haircut in the adjacent store, but we rarely saw him. Nevertheless, if the club was dirty, John told us immediately.

Mike Lucci, a former linebacker for the Detroit Lions, joined the company. For the past few years, Don Wildman had taken about 100 top people to the Super Bowl, on an all-expense-paid trip. Lucci had inspired Don to run these contests, because it always doubled the grosses for that period and since Lucci was a former NFL player, he always got great seats to the game at a good price. Several months into my management at Little Neck, they announced that new sales contest.

The members at Little Neck could be at times difficult, if the services weren't working at 100 percent, which often happened. For example, if the whirlpool was out, it could take a day to get it fixed and during that time, angry customers would come knocking at my door.

In the first few weeks of my leadership, I experienced a few of these knocks when I had potential customers in my office—which of course made it more difficult to sign them up.

One day I had a brainstorm. I had my sales trainee take my office, while I took the sales trainee office, which faced the front desk. This was perfect. The front desk was where all the business happened. This was where the phones rang with new business and where people walked in and asked for membership. Why in the world would any manager want to be stuck behind closed doors on the other side of the lobby and miss all this action? I told the trainee if members came to the door, he or she was to handle the situation by inviting them into the office, close the door and hear their complaint. I told the trainee this was part of the management trainee program. The change worked nicely—in fact, so nicely that when I told some of the members that I was the manager, they thought I was joking and then I had to get one of the staff to confirm that I was the person in charge. The club was huge and I had to get big numbers, so I did what was best for the club and what was best

38

for me.

During this period, we were doing a renewal drive and on an hourly basis, I would make announcements to the club at large to try to renew the members. The renewal drive was going well, but some of the members wanted an additional six months and the only way to give it to them was to say it was a reward for recommending other guests who had joined. Wanting to get to a Superbowl, I started giving this extra time under the table, and some members were walking away with two years' membership instead of one.

News got around that this was a good offer, and between the new sales I was pulling in, and the back-end sales, I was one of the leaders going to the Super Bowl.

Out of the 100 tickets that were designated for the winners, 15 of them were for the New York market, including the top brass. That year, 1983, I got to go to Pasadena, Calif. to see the Washington Redskins play the Miami Dolphins.

The night before the game, Don Wildman arranged for all 100 of us to attend a black-tie dinner with a dance band that played songs from the American Songbook.

Buses picked us up and took us to the Santa Monica Pier to the restaurant, which had a terrific ocean view. I was 28 years old and life couldn't have been better, because I considered these guys and gals my family. When you're a manager, you work 10 to 10, Monday through Friday and when you work 60 hours a week, you know everything about your colleagues. You know whom they are dating, their favorite foods, actors, movies, colors.

Don Wildman was always a top-shelf guy. During halftime, a plane flew over the field in Pasadena, and wrote in the sky, "Happy 50th Birthday Don Wildman." I leaned over to the colleague next to me, Howard Friedberg, and I said to him, "Everyone in the stadium is saying, 'Who is Don Wildman?' That's our boss, right, Howard?"

We had seats at the Miami end zone. When you see my photos, you would think I had a zoom lens: that was how close to the action I was. The final score of Super Bowl XVII was Redskins 27, Dolphins 17.

By the time I returned from the Super Bowl trip, the main office had gotten the drift that I had been a little too generous in giving members more time on their memberships. I got a visit from John Wilton one afternoon. He said, "Pack your stuff, you're being transferred. You're going to Woodbridge."

"Woodbridge? That's New Jersey! Why?"

He told me what the main office had discovered. Obviously, the company thought it was a big deal that I had given some members extra time to get the gross. And on this one, they wanted to hang me out to dry.

I was going to follow John there in my car, and he said, "Oh no, you're driving with me."

"What about my car?"

"I'll drive you back later tonight."

"John, you finish taking your numbers at 11:00."

"I know, and that's when I will return you to Little Neck."

There I was in Woodbridge, New Jersey: a Brooklyn boy who was accustomed to finding a delicatessen on every corner. Now, on my hour lunch break, it took me 20 minutes to drive to get a sandwich and 20 minutes more to return. I had no time to work out anymore and I knew if I did well in Woodbridge, the company would never transfer me. The next week I bought the book *War And Peace*, by Leo Tolstoy, and I called my assistant manager into my office. I told him, "If you do what I tell you, you will be a manager."

He said, "Sure, what?"

I said, "You are going to run the club, while I read this book. They won't keep me here if I am not producing. They are just wasting me. You do well, and when it comes time for me to leave, I will tell them you are ready to manage." My assistant agreed and I shook his hand.

For the next 30 days, Leo Tolstoy and I became good friends. Just as I was about to finish the book, I got the call. I felt like a minor league pitcher waiting to go to the majors. John said, "Ok, we are transferring you."

"Where?"

"Madison Avenue." Which is another name for the Winslow Hotel.

"I start tomorrow?"

"Yeah."

Before he hung up, I said, "John, this guy Chris, my assistant, is great."

"Yeah, I know. We are making him the manager." He also warned me not to pull any "Mickey" stuff anymore. The company had an expression. When you "did a Mickey," it was short for Mickey Mouse. It meant you gave members more time than they deserved. Trust me, the company closed its eyes most of the time and took the cash. This was a regular practice. But it was against government regulations to favor one member over another, and I think every now and then the company had to go on record as having punished someone. Once Harry got wind from the members, it was my turn to go into the monkey barrel. Either way, I served my time and was onto the next gym. I was excited. Madison Avenue was a daytime club and that was when you did all your sales. It was quiet at night compared to a club like Little Neck where most of the sales came in the evening.

The former Winslow Hotel was being converted into an office building. We didn't close the gym during the period while the building was in full construction mode. The members kept coming—even with cinder blocks falling through the ceiling and mice and rats crossing the exercise gym floor while a class was in session.

One day, the air conditioner went out and stayed broken for weeks. The mirrors would fog, because the whirlpool in the basement was throwing off heat. The members couldn't see themselves. I called John, to see if he would allow me to turn off the whirlpool. He said, "I forbid you. I already have members calling me about the air conditioning; I don't need the members calling me about the whirlpool too."

Harry arrived on a Saturday, when I had the day off, and decreed that the club looked filthy, with mirrors in which members couldn't see themselves. The following day was the supervisors' meeting, held at the Park Lane Hotel. At the beginning of the meeting, Harry announced he had a new award that he was going to institute that day and that he would hand it out later in the meeting. Everyone in the room got excited because they loved getting recognition from Harry. He would always give out the manager of the month awards and right after the last one was handed out, he would say, "These awards can either be your stepping stone or tombstone." knowing how some managers could get big-headed and lazy after receiving the award.

After coffee was served, Harry stood up behind the podium, there were about twenty people present at this long oval table. He announced the winner, which was my supervisor at the Winslow Hotel. My supervisor was ecstatic and happily trotted up to get his award. He was a tall lanky guy that loved to jog and had barely any body fat on him. Now Harry shook his hand and he slipped out a brand-new corrugated box from under the podium and started to open it. Before he took out the item, he announced that the award goes to my supervisor "who has the filthiest club in the system." My supervisor's face went pale. Harry took out a brand-new toilet bowl seat, opened it up and placed it around my supervisor's neck. He was mortified. He then shook his hand and said, "Congratulations!"

Monday could not come quick enough for my supervisor and at 10:00 A.M., I received a phone call and I got my guts handed to me. I tried to tell him it wasn't my fault. The club was in a full-blown construction site with no air conditioning. He would have none of that, saying my club was the dirtiest in the system. I explained that I had reported the situation to John, and John would not take my recommendation to shut off the whirlpool that kept the mirrors steamed up. But my supervisor kept browbeating me. This went on for about 10 to 15 minutes till finally I said, "Howard, go fuck yourself," and hung up.

For the next two days, it was quiet and on Wednesday evening John came into the club. Shortly thereafter, my supervisor arrived and went into another office and closed the door. I knew my day of reckoning had come. John pulled me into the office he was occupying and told me he wanted me to apologize to my Howard and I refused. John persisted, and I realized my position was in jeopardy. Therefore, I finally agreed, thinking this would give me a reprieve and then they would leave me alone. I knocked on the door. Howard opened it. I didn't enter the office. I was standing outside. I said, "I apologize."

He just said, "Okay."

I went back into my office.

At the end of the next evening, John transferred me out of his area. It was a huge transfer. I would no longer work for him. The regional area had about 26 locations at this point, divided into two areas. John had half of them and Steve Mekuly had the other half. John told me I was going to Howard Friedberg's club, which was part of Mekuly's area. Howard Friedberg was notoriously tough to work for. He was known to blow people out. I felt John made this move hoping that Howard Friedberg would eventually fire me. However, unbeknownst to John, I had become friends with Howard on two company trips we had taken together, one to Fort Lauderdale and the other to the Super Bowl in Pasadena which I mentioned earlier.

I immediately telephoned Howard and told him I was coming to his group. He had been informed already; he welcomed me aboard. I pledged my allegiance to him and Steve Mekuly. I told him that I would work night and day to show the others that they made a mistake.

I told Howard that I felt they would like for him to blow me out—and if he did, John and my former supervisor would win. Howard liked hearing this, and that's how I started to be on his team.

The next day I arrived at Sutton Place. It was a cozy club, not co-ed. Women came on Monday, Wednesday, and Fridays and men came on the other days. Prior to Jack La Lanne taking over, it had been a European Health Club.

The staff was great. They were friendly, and the members were just as nice. Most of the members lived nearby. The club was located on First Avenue and 55th Street.

Howard and I were happy working together. He gave me all the support I needed. I started listening to the conference calls that Steve would give in the morning. His style was similar to that of Vince Lombardi, the greatest coach in the history of professional American football.

After Steve would finish revving up his managers—there were about 10 on the line—he would ask us to pledge a number that our club would do for that day and everybody would give a number, depending on the size of the club. He made you make a mental note and set a goal. On close-outs, the numbers would quadruple.

After about two weeks into my new position, the police raided the Winslow Hotel, my previous club. It appeared that Hector, the locker room attendant, had a side gig. He was selling large volumes of cocaine and crack and now I understood why so many of the lockers in the locker room were off-limits, locked with his locks. That was where he kept his stash and why he had so many friends that came to visit who were not members.

Once again, I thanked my lucky stars for not being there when the police raided. I knew they might have arrested me as well for being the manager.

A new sale was about to begin, and it was called MEGA, which stood for Member Enrollment Grand Awards. This sale involved giving members big incentives if they brought in other new members. They were giving managers and the salesmen big incentives too. Every one of the sales-staff could increase their salary by 25, 50 or 100 percent if they hit certain gross sales numbers for the club. They also gave out two 940 Porsches to first place clubs in the country. At this point the company had three (300) hundred locations. One car would be for the highest percent of sales over their quota; the other for the highest cash percentage over the quota. They used the two different standards because a small club couldn't compete with a larger club on a cash basis.

Howard and I worked terrifically together and I knew he had my back. Once a year Harry used to give out two-week passes to the members, and I convinced Howard to give me a large corrugated box of yellow two-week passes. We just started handing these out at the desk. I was the first manager to do this in the chain outside of the normal time frame. Soon the gym had plenty of guests enjoying the facilities. I told my staff not to pressure anyone to join and let them simply enjoy the services for two weeks—then at the end, sit them down and see if they would like to join. Sure, enough, that strategy worked.

At the end of the contest, we didn't double our salary, but we went 50 percent above. I was pleased with my accomplishment, especially since my previous supervisor from the Winslow Hotel had been looking to get me out of the company by sending me to Howard Friedberg's team.

Now that I had done so well at Sutton Place, I got a call at 10:00 one night, concerning a new location at Broadway and 75th Street. The famed Fairway Supermarket was located at the base of the block. I was to replace the first manager, whose name was Sid. He had been there for the entire year doing the pre-sale. A pre-sale is when you are allowed to sell memberships during the construction period. The State of New York grants you the right to sell memberships prior to the opening. The company must post a hefty bond before you can bring in the first dollar. The sales pitch is usually done in a trailer outside a club, but in

Manhattan, a parked trailer is almost impossible, so instead a few offices are installed within the premises, along with colored drawings from the architect's office depicting what the location will look like.

Managers loved to work a pre-sale because whatever ads ran in print and on TV would always include a sidebar that the new location was about to open along with the address. This direct marketing promotion immediately brought sales to the new location. The real test for the manager was to see if the sales remained high once the location opened.

On the first day I arrived, I doubled the sales. As soon as I had entered the club, I made sure the desk was manned properly. A well-maintained desk can be the success or failure of any club. The receptionist should be courteous, but firm, and should not let any of the members in without showing their cards and signing in. Receptionists should be gracious and greet everyone in an equally pleasant manner. The receptionist is the eyes and ears of the manager and sales staff.

I started holding morning meetings with the staff to go over the presentation and all the points to touch upon to produce a closing deal. I would demonstrate how to get a prospect to commit to getting in shape that very day, and not put it off for another time. Having had two parents who died of heart attacks, I had no guilt in persuading someone to join, then and there to get themselves healthier. Sales immediately went up.

Often on my break, I would use the Nautilus equipment that was set up for circuit training. Circuit training had 12 machines that were lined up in a straight line. There was a clock and a recording. Every 30 seconds, one would do eight to 12 reps of an exercise; then the recording would say, "Stop, rotate." Then it was off to the next machine. Circuit training increases muscle strength, enhances joint flexibility, improves cardiovascular function, and helps weight loss. I also kept my bike at work and on my breaks, I sometimes rode to Central Park and would cycle within the park's loop for six miles.

I became friends with Murray Zborowski, a member. He saw how much I enjoyed cycling and encouraged me to get a better bike. He introduced me to Lenny, who owned a Toga bike shop not far away. When I met Lenny, he told me how the folks from Sprite soda had just been there and that they were looking for "an Italian type" to do a TV commercial. I thought that Lenny would say anything to sell me a bike, not believing him, and I laughed to myself. He asked me what my budget was and I said, "Four hundred dollars."

I was about to leave, but he said, "Wait, I gotta call the producer." I realized he was telling the truth, and sure enough, he called the producer and made an appointment for me to do a Go - See. A Go -See is a Hollywood expression of an audition. Prior to walking out the door, always being grateful, I told Lenny that whatever I made on the commercial I would apply to the bike.

A few days went by and I showed up at Steve Horn Productions. I later found out that Steve did all the "I Love New York" commercials. I arrived in full cyclist attire. I was sporting my Shimano shirt with my skins, which are those tight cyclist pants with a camisole cushion in the seat. I also had on a hat that said Campagnolo. They filmed my audition with my bangs hanging out of the hat. They asked me to say, "Buona Fortuna." which means good luck in Italian. I said it several times. Steve Laughed, saying "You sound like a New Yorker" and then he added, "We can always dub his voice."

The following day, I got a call from wardrobe, warning me that they weren't supposed to call before confirmation, but what were the sizes of my waist, shirt, and hat?

The following week, I got the official call that I had the job. They took me and four other actors to upstate New York and filmed us on the side of a mountain at the edge of a vineyard. I made $600 for that day and as promised, I went back and applied that sum to my $400, to make my bicycle budget $1,000. Lenny and I went on to build a custom bike together. I still own it today. It is amazing. The frame is made from

Columbus SL tubing made by Zullo and the weight is a mere 16 lbs. That is super light for a bike. The gears shift and all the mechanicals were made by Campagnolo. This is the best of the best for components. Lenny and I chose an Avocet seat and Cinelli handlebars and the color is cherry red.

After the commercial, I thought this may have been my new career and immediately found a commercial photographer called Mario and did a shooting.

Twenty years ago, this bike was priced by another shop owner at $25,000. I wish that every one of my investments multiplied by 25.

I got to go to the annual gathering called the Consortium, held in Los Angeles in 1983. I was one of 300 attendees from all over the country: another black- tie event, where they hand out awards for top-grossing clubs and profitability. New York won all the awards that year and it was a special moment when all our top brass and managers from the New York area were holding silver trophies the size of the Stanley Cup.

J. Walter Thompson was our ad agency, and they announced our spokesperson for the year. The year before it had been Raquel Welch. This year it was going to be Jaclyn Smith from *Charlie's Angels*, and she was there.

On the first day of the Consortium, they announced they would be having a "tin-can triathlon." The swim would be held in Marina del Rey Bay. It would be a quarter (¼) mile open-water swim, with a 25-mile bike ride along a concrete pathway on the beach facing the water, and finally a 10-kilometer run. They were supplying the bikes and if you finished the race, they shipped the bike to your home.

Howard Friedberg and I, who were best buddies, now entered. Harry came over to me the night before at a dinner he threw for his group from New York at the Spaghetti Factory and said in front of everyone, "I hear you entered the race. I don't care about you winning, but you can't quit. If you enter, you've got to finish."

I said, "No problem, I won't quit and I'll finish." I felt I would do well since I worked out and swam every day.

The next day was the race. One hundred of us jumped into the ice-cold water of Marina del Rey and soon I found myself struggling—not being used to an open water swim, since I only practiced in the pools in the gyms. Once in the water, I now saw male lifeguards sitting on surfboards. They were there if you needed assistance. But soon I realized that I was on my own since the men were only helping the female swimmers. The swimming path was clear; there were 20 orange buoys in a straight line and you had to swim down one aisle, then turn and come back. Once I finished the swim, I needed help getting out of the water. I then ran to the bike. Prior to the race, you placed your t-shirt, shorts, sneakers and socks by your bike that was numbered. Now, once you changed, you were off for the 25-mile bike ride. It was a beautiful sunny day and there was no humidity. Halfway into my ride, I saw people returning from the other direction. These were people who had already finished the swim and half of the bike race and had now turned and were coming back to the base to start their run. Don Wildman was leading the pack, but that didn't discourage me. I could only think of what Harry said about not quitting. I felt as though I was in Rome with gladiators. These weren't regular people; these were super people with super strength.

I finished the bike ride and now for the run. I ran and never stopped. I felt as if I stopped even once I was finished. I ran at my own pace and at times, I looked like one of those runners at the end of a marathon. I was running, but one could see I was in some pain.

I was about to finish the race, and in the distance I saw a crowd of people standing around exercise equipment. These were the same machines that the health clubs had. I said to myself, "Oh no, now they want me to do a complete circuit of lifting weights." which included leg extension, pull down, bench press, bicep curls. etc., etc. I was exhausted, but I finished the weight lifting portion of the race and I completed the race. Soon thereafter, I learned that I came in last place. I was discouraged to hear the news, until I heard that there were many people who had quit along the way. That immediately made me feel better.

Harry took the group out to dinner that night and I could not lift my arms from the swim. Harry came over to me. Howard Friedberg and Audie Ward, who also did the race, were sitting next to me. Harry said, "I heard you guys finished. Congratulations."

I said, "Yeah, but I was in last place."

He stopped, looked me dead in the eye and said, "But you finished, and that's what matters most."

Lesson learned and the moral of the story: if you say you are going to do something, do it and don't give up.

The annual New York black-tie event always took place in October and we were back at the Pierre Hotel. They had invited Joe Girard as the keynote speaker. Joe Girard is listed in *The Guinness World Book of Records* as selling the most automobiles of anyone in the world in a single year. So here we were at dinner, 300 of us. About 75 percent of us were male, aged 20 to 30 years. There was enough testosterone in the room to fill an aquarium.

Joe started his speech and the crowd perked up. Then, suddenly, Joe jumped on the dais, which was about 40 feet long, walking quickly back and forth over plates, forks, knives, and glasses. Place settings fell off the table. As he revved up the troops, he started taking off his clothes from the waist up. First, the jacket that he swung around his head, then his suspenders, shirt, and tie. As he swung all his clothes above his head, he started yelling at the top of his voice, *"We're number one! We're number one! We're number one!"* He jumped off the front of the table facing the audience and started jumping up and down again, chanting more of the same and telling everyone to join in. Three hundred young people did and what a thunderous sound it was.

Everyone was standing up and jumping up and down shouting, *"We're number one! We're number one! We're number one!"* The floor started to tremble; and the main chandelier shook over the tables. I said, "Oh my goodness, the chandelier is going to fall and kill these people." Luckily, it didn't.

The following day at 9:01 A.M., Harry got a call from the general manager at the Pierre, he was French of course. He said, "Mr. Schwartz, how did you and your company enjoy yourself last night?"

Harry said, "It was a wonderful evening and unforgettable."

The manager said, "I am pleased everyone had a good time." He reminded Harry that their contract was for the next three years. He then told him that unfortunately he must cancel it. He followed by saying; "Mr. Schwartz, this is the Pierre Hotel and all that yelling and screaming was unacceptable." The manager wished Harry good luck. For the next quarterly meeting the company now moved to the Park Lane Hotel on Central Park South which is only a few blocks away from The Pierre. The Park Lane was facing Central Park north, rather than west. To that point, we had only used the Park Lane for small meetings but now we were forced to use their ballroom. Once the meeting opened, Harry announced that this was our new venue and we all should be orderly and act as ladies and gentlemen. Of course, Harry said that with a big grin on his face.

The company was running fast and furious. By now, Don Wildman had sold the company to Bally and the new company was called Bally Fitness. Wildman signed a five-year management agreement by which he stayed on running it with all the partners, Harry included. In the new management contract, if the executives hit certain cash gross levels over the next five years, they would all get a 30 percent kicker above what they got on the sale. My managerial position now had been moved to the Fort Lee, New Jersey location when this took place. The club's names were eventually to be changed to Bally Fitness, I believed it was going to take a few years to ease the new name into the system.

During this time, Fort Lee was in the last place for profitability. Michael, who was the manager there for years, had the best bookkeeping and the cleanest club. I had worked with Michael prior, at Kings Highway, and I knew he loved to work out several hours a day, keeping his physique in top form. He also had a car that he waxed several times a week. Michael went to Military school and was very disciplined.

When I arrived to replace him, my strategy was to focus the staff on sales and service, besides cleaning. I was not worried about the place staying clean because everyone was in the habit of keeping every inch spotless. All I had to do was get everyone to sell and service too.

All the hard work finally paid off, and within a year's time, I was informed (in a casual conversation, by my area director, Bill Milburn) that Forth Less had placed in the number-two position for profitability. By now the New York area had 40 clubs. I had taken the last-place club in profitability—which they were planning to close and relocate—and with my sales and management techniques, moved it to the number-two position. I didn't realize at the time what an accomplishment that was, because all I was interested in doing was having the next good week in sales.

What happened next was inevitable. I leased a brand new 1984 BMW 320i and took my then-girlfriend, a gal from Trento, Italy, to Canada for a week. We had a great time driving and visiting Montreal, Quebec City staying at the famed Frontenac Hotel overseeing The Saint Lawrence River, Toronto, and Niagara Falls on the Canadian side. It was a five speed which I just learned to drive and I had fun driving it.

I returned to learn that my assistant manager, David, had doubled my gross from the previous week. We found out a year later he gave the house away to get those numbers, but when that happened, Steve started to give me hell on the conference calls with the other supervisors. Managers only attended the 10:00 A.M. conference call, but if you were a supervisor or senior manager like me, you had to be on one more one-hour call. In total, I was off the selling floor 10 to 15 hours a week. I tried to explain to Steve why David was beating my weekly sales, because I was on these calls. My contemporaries were listening, but Steve wouldn't have it and told me to get off the call because this would be the last time I was on a supervisor's call. Well, once again, I made someone angry, and I was back in the doghouse.

III. THE VERTICAL CLUB

Two days later I got called to the main office in Rockville Centre, Long Island. Steve had a "judge desk": a tall desk, which he stood behind. When you are in front, you are looking upwards to the speaker and you feel like you're being sentenced.

Steve told me, "I am transferring you to the Vertical Club. Tommy Di Natale needs help and I asked him which one of my managers he wanted, and he selected you."

I had sent Tommy a model toy car of the Porsche 940, wishing him luck to win the MEGA contest we had had earlier in the year. I had sent it along with a nice note—and now I was sorry that I had done that, since it meant I had made a bond with Tommy that was going to cost me my management.

I said, "Steve, I am about to make $50,000 this year as a manager. That's the most I ever made." This was October, 1984. I played the goal card, knowing how much getting to a goal meant to Steve. Steve stayed quiet and then said, "What if I guarantee you $1,000 a week for the rest of the year to help Tommy?" I thought about it. I knew this was Tommy's domain and anyone who went there in the past never made it, but I saw a spark of possibility, where just maybe I could get a chance to figure out how to run The Vertical Club.

The Vertical Club was our highest-end club. It catered to the upper echelon. It was over 100,000 square feet with six tennis courts and eight squash courts, with a 20,000-square-foot-gym floor fully equipped with a suspended running track that went around the circumference of the gym floor. Arnold Schwarzenegger and Billy Jean King were often seen there, along with a young Kathleen Turner.

The next day I arrived at the Vertical Club and for the next six months I felt as though I had been sentenced to purgatory. It was clear Tommy ran the ship. All my managerial duties were stripped; I was just a salesman and for some reason, I couldn't sell these people. They did not wish to listen to the canned presentation that I had performed for the past eight years. The other three salespeople did well, but I could not get myself arrested.

Don Imus the famous radio jock, was a member and a daily visitor; so was Chuck Barris, host of *The Gong Show*. Rusty Staub, the old Mets ballplayer, ran the restaurant called Rusty's. The only star I had previously met at Jack La Lanne's was the dancer Gwen Verdon, when I ran the club on Broadway and 75th Street.

This was my eighth year in the company, and I knew that since I had made Steve angry, there was no returning to Jack La Lanne. I started thinking about leaving my health club family.

I thought about real estate. I remember a story my mom told me when I was a child: One summer's day, my father came home to a seven- course turkey meal with all the trimmings. Since this was in the early 1950s, there was no air conditioning. My father knew something was up. He said to my mom, "Okay, Annie, what did you buy?" thinking she bought a dress, or a radio.

She smiled and said, "A three-family house."

Dad just about spit his food out.

"We can't afford that! I'm only a longshoreman."

Mom said, "Sure we can." She sat down next to him and with pencil and paper, she showed him how they would rent out the top floor and first floor and get a mortgage—and with his salary, they would get a mortgage and live rent free. I think she gave him that night to decide. They did buy that house and as years went by, they kept on buying bigger and better properties. At one point, they owned three at once. This was when they were both living. I made up my mind I was going into real estate like my parents—but I had to figure out how to do that.

IV. STARTING MY REAL ESTATE CAREER

Judith Grey was married to a famous radio announcer, Joel Grey. She was a member of the European/Jack LaLanne Health Club that I previously managed, near the Vertical Club where I was now working. I called her to see if she could help me, I told her I wanted to move into real estate. She arranged for me to meet Gail Coverdale. Gail was a residential real estate broker who knew a lot of people in the industry. I met with them over dinner. Gail explained the different aspects of real estate. She said that real estate has different specialties: residential rentals and sales, and commercial, which had many more choices. She explained that in commercial real estate there was office leasing, where you dealt mainly with corporations; then there were building sales where you dealt with investors and developers. I thought selling buildings and development sounded interesting, so she arranged for me to meet the office manager, Mark Sands, at a new firm called Siegal Shor & Associates, located on Fifth Avenue in the Flatiron District.

I went to see Mark—and shortly thereafter, I got the job. I gave notice to Steve Mekuly. Harry called up a few weeks later and tried to woo me back and when he saw he couldn't, he offered me a letter of recommendation. I thought that was nice of him and although I turned him down at first, I called his secretary Nancy Terra the following day, to say I would be happy to receive the letter. Several weeks later, John Wilton sent me a beautiful letter stating that maybe my resignation was just a sabbatical and that one day I might return to a position equal to, or above, the one I had left.

Mark was a good manager, training me on the mechanics of the business of investment sales. You must be good with numbers in constantly looking at the ROI, which is the return on investment, and F.A.R., the floor area ratio, which is a calculation you use to determine how many square feet you can build. If your property has a 10 F.A.R., and the plot size is 10,000 square feet, you can build 100,000 square feet in total. Part of being an investment sales broker is to constantly look for good deals and offer them to your customer. Scouting for a good deal is like looking for a needle in a haystack.

In my first two years, I sold three (3) twenty-four (24) unit apartment buildings in Harlem to different investors. This is when Harlem first started getting hot. Then a half-acre piece of land in Long Beach, Long Island. My buyer / developer hired an architect and got approvals to build 18 townhouses, which he then sold and flipped the contract. Soon I was involved with a team in selling a 200,000-square-foot property in Maspeth, Queens. It was an industrial building and I got credit for finding the property. Then in my third year, I moved to a company called First National Realty and started working on selling properties on a national level. Then I moved to Stephen Brener's office, which only sold hotels. Brener was the hotel guru who founded the legendary NYU Hospitality conference that received 4,000 professionals a year at the Marriott Marquis in Times Square. He gave me a draw of $500 a week. Selling hotels was more difficult than the other investment properties. I thought my experience of selling properties and running health clubs would help me to sell a consumer business like hotels. It was, but hotels were still a different animal. I realized it was going to take a while to understand this new business model.

Over the past three years I had depleted my savings. I had started with $25,000 in my savings account and now I was heavily in debt. To supplement my income, I asked Gail Coverdale if I could work weekends renting apartments at her store on Third Avenue and 95th Street in Manhattan. She agreed.

On Saturday mornings, before we got busy, I would go see six of the latest apartments to learn the stock, then I would rush to the office. Gail ran ads in the *New York Times* and by 10:30 the calls would start to come in. Here's how I would rent apartments. I would meet the prospect at her store and qualify them. Since I would have already seen a handful of one- and two-bedroom apartments that morning, I would have some idea of the inventory. I would take the prospect to see vacant apartments in their size and budget range. If it was a couple, I would show them an apartment and if I saw they had some interest, I would say, "Okay, I am going to wait outside the apartment and you both talk. When you finish, I'll be waiting for you."

It always worked. I knew if I didn't give them private time to discuss, they would have to go home to talk. Once they opened the door, if they weren't smiling, I would just take them to the next apartment and do the same thing over and over till they found an apartment they liked. In my short time with Gail, I always rented at least one apartment a weekend, and sometimes two. Lesson learned. If you can, give your customer some time to talk about an apartment they saw before they go to the next one or prior to them leaving and going home and get feedback if they still didn't find the perfect location..

After three years of hitting the pavement in New York City and then nationally, I missed running the health clubs and my old cronies. I was burnt out from working six to seven days a week. I thought I was destined to go back to the health club industry, but little did I know you can never go back. By then I had run up $50,000 in charge card debt by using 17 cards. Back then, they would just practically mail you a card with a substantial amount on it. That was huge indebtedness in 1988. I decided to file for bankruptcy—even though I had sold those 24-unit apartment buildings in Harlem at the beginning of a bull market. The commissions were miniscule, because the properties traded at $150,000 apiece. I sold them at one and a half (1 ½ 's) times the rent roll. At that price it meant the rent in those buildings was $100,000 at the time. Now, the rent roll must be $1,000,000 and those buildings are probably selling at eight (8'x's) times rent roll giving the property value of $8 million dollars. Those property owners got great deals. I sold one to a fireman friend, Michael Labarbera, and he sold the property a year later and doubled his money. However, if he had held onto it, over the next 30 years he would have made millions as my calculations just demonstrated.

The land I sold gave me a $15,000 commission and the industrial building I was part of was a small commission too. I got the experience, but the big money hadn't yet arrived.

V. RETURNING TO THE HEALTH CLUBS

I made a call to Steve Mekuly at Jack La Lanne's and two weeks later I was back in the gym business, hoping that I would be happy, but I was not. With all the freedom I had experienced in the previous three years, I couldn't stay inside a gym from 10 to 10 every day, and as soon as I got back, I started planning my exit again—the way Papillon did when he got caught escaping prison for the first time and immediately planned his escape for a second. Steve McQueen played that part very well in the movie along with Dustin Hoffman both playing prisoners on an isolated island with huge waves that McQueen finally figured a way to harness to complete his escape.

I realized the letter of recommendation that was written three years prior assuring me of a position of equal or better stature had expired and it was either Harry or Steve that wanted to make an example of me. Well they did, because all my new assignments were always 100 miles from home. This meant I had to leave home at 8:00 A.M. to open the club at 10, and I would not get home till 1:00 the next morning. Those were my hours from Monday through Friday and on the close-outs, you were now expected to work the weekends to help the assistant manager.

I also had a shopping center in Salem, Mass. that I was trying to sell as a real estate salesperson. That deal started when I was at First National Realty and then followed me to my next company with Stephen Brener, and now that I was back at Jack La Lanne's, it started to grow legs. I am now stationed in Pearl River, N.Y. at a facility that used to be European Health clubs, that we took over and rebranded it to Jack La Lanne's. Everyday I travel from Brooklyn, one and a half hours. The seller was Butcher and Singer, an investment banking firm from Philadelphia, and the buyer was a local property owner from Salem, Massachusetts. I arranged for the sellers to meet the buyer in Salem, the following week. When they arrived, for some reason, the buyer did not want to meet them. I found this to be a strange way to negotiate. I went to his office and nicely said, "How can you do this to people, they flew in from Philadelphia to meet you?"

He said, "I don't care," and rattled off something about his proposal. He really had no explanation. But, I knew he was the right buyer. My point person at Butcher and Singer was Jim Stanton and he was upset; so was I. I had worked on this deal for months and I had just driven five hours from Brooklyn (and would have to drive five hours back) to hear this. The following day, I called Jim and asked him who was the biggest property owner in Boston. He immediately answered, "Harold Brown." I told Jim not to count my guy out yet.

I called the buyer and said, "Do you know of Harold Brown?

Michael, the buyer, said, "Why?"

I said, "Jim said he is looking to buy the mall."

Suddenly, my buyer's voice went into a high pitch.

He retorted, "Hell, Harold Brown doesn't need financing, he can just write a check... Joe, I will call you right back."

Thirty minutes later, he called me.

"Okay, I agree to the price of $3 million and I'll put a $100,000 deposit down at the contract, and I'll close in 90 days."

I said, "Fine, I'll call you right back." I called Jim and told him what I had done. We had a good laugh and he accepted the deal. I did this while I was dressed in my company's dark blue tracksuit with logos on the jacket and pants.

Afterwards, the buyer told me he needed this site for an assemblage he was putting together. Like I said, I knew he was the right buyer.

Lesson learned: Know when to bluff.

Now with this deal pending, I had to figure a way to get out of the gym business. I put together my résumé and I thought I was clever: I scripted two. One had a break with my leaving Jack La Lanne and going into real estate; the other didn't have my leaving at all. I thought, "Who would know?" Once the two résumés were completed, I started reaching out.

One headhunter immediately offered me a job to run a business school in the Bronx. It paid $50,000 a year and 10 percent of the pre- tax profit. I said, "Sure that sounds good."

The following week I went to the Bronx and had the interview; it went well. The gentleman liked one of my expressions: "Inspect, don't expect."

The next week I got the offer. Immediately, I called the other headhunters to tell them not to send my résumé out anymore. One head-hunter asked me to describe the job, and like a fool I did. One hour later, the headhunter who had made me the offer called and said, "A résumé just came across his desk." Have I ever worked in real estate? I said I had, with an explanation, and he nicely said, "Yeah, but you lied." and politely rescinded the offer.

Years later, this same business school got fined $25 million for tax evasion. That was another bullet I dodged—knowing that if I had been the general manager there, I would have been associated with their wrongdoing. Lesson learned, know when to thank your blessings.

It was 1988 and the total commission was $90,000 for the shopping center in Salem, Massachusetts. But then there were deductions. I had to pay half to the broker; then there was the draw that they gave me and the 10 percent I had to give to the manager, who supposedly helped me close the deal, but really the deal closed itself. One had to be at the closing to pick up the check, or this time the check was mailed. With those deductions figured in, I came out with $15,000. Anyone else would have bought a car and been happy to be back at the old job, but not me.

I made up my mind to leave the gym business when my car engine seized and I had no way to get to and from work. I stayed unemployed for about five months. I hated not working. So, I took a job as a sales-person at a business school and found myself selling courses in bank telling, word processing, and security programs to inner-city teenagers and 20 somethings. The government gave school loans and it seemed like an easy sale, but I was the worst salesman at the school. I just couldn't convince these potential students to join that day. The place where I worked was Barclay Career School, located in Manhattan on Park Avenue South in the low 30s. There was a nice clothing store a few blocks away and with the extra money I had in my pocket I invested in three good suits, six shirts, and ties to match.

One Sunday, I saw an ad in the paper for a job in real estate—a canvass-er—and it paid a salary. It had something to do with retail. I thought that might be perfect: I had been a retailer for eight years and I had worked with property owners for three years selling them properties. I knew both sides of the table well. I never thought I would have an opportunity to go back into real estate and now I had another chance. I called the number, and asked for Lee Stand.

"Mr. Stand, this is Joe Aquino, and I am calling about the canvasser's job in the New York *Times*."

"Today is Wednesday. That ad came out on Sunday. The job has been filled."

"Mr. Stand, I think you really want to meet me. I just sold a 90,000 square foot shopping center in Salem, Mass. I also sold three apartment buildings in Harlem, and a half-acre of land in Long Beach. I was also part of the sale of a big industrial building in Maspeth. You really want to meet me."

That Friday, I arrived at Mr. Stand's office. In the background the radio was softly playing "Gonna Fly Now," from the movie *Rocky*. I saw it as a good sign.

The interview started and I showed Lee Stand a professional shot of the shopping mall I had just sold that cost me $700.00 that I had done by a professional photographer in Salem. Digital photography wasn't invented yet and that's how much it cost me to get the mall shot. I made the investment knowing that just telling someone about the sale would not be the same as seeing an actual professional photo.

The idea worked, Lee liked the photo and started pitching me to continue selling properties and doing investment sales. He offered me a desk. I politely declined since the recent tax laws changed a property owner's valuation by 30 percent downward and all the property owners planned to hold onto their buildings for the next few years till the valuations went higher. The tax change put the industry in a slack market. In a slack market, the properties do not move because the prices dropped and you cannot make any commissions. I told Lee I wanted the canvasser's job. I was pitching as though I were going for the company's CEO position. I knew I could do this.

Lee said, "I gave it to a kid who just graduated college."

"Mr. Stand, that fellow can get a job anywhere. You want to give it to me, a guy who has experience."

Lee paused and finally said, "All right, I can't make that decision. Let me talk to the owner and call me next Tuesday."

The following Tuesday arrived and I was at the business school. (This was prior to cell phones becoming ubiquitous.) I went to the corner, put a quarter in the public phone, and punched in the number.

"Mr. Stand, hi. It's Joe Aquino. We met last week in your office. This is about the canvasser's job. "

"Well." Mr. Stand paused and said, "well" again. My heart was thumping. "Well, we decided to give you a shot, we are giving you the job. We told the kid to find something else." I immediately shouted out, "Mr. Stand, you will not be sorry you hired me, I'll make you proud of me. "

I went back to the business school and quit my job. I went around the entire school thanking everyone for the opportunity they had given me and everyone wished me luck. I was so happy that I was returning to real estate. I had a few bucks in the bank by now. I lived in a furnished basement apartment in Manhattan Beach, paying only $600 a month including utilities. I was a half block from the water. I was happy and on my way.

VI. RETURNING TO REAL ESTATE

It was my first day back in real estate leasing: March, 1989, at a company called Garrick Aug Associates Store Leasing Inc. They had 10,000 square feet on the fourth floor at 99 Park Avenue in Midtown. All the managers had offices on the periphery, with windows, and the rest of the salesmen were in the middle, which they called the bullpen. The bullpen had no tall walls. The walls were about three feet in height and everyone had a clear view of everyone else. It looked like the old newsrooms you would see in a movie.

Charles Aug was the owner and everybody called him Charlie. He was a tall, fully stocked man who looked like the actor George Kennedy. He wore thin horn-rim glasses, was partially bald and had a deep baritone voice. Aug was the surviving partner. We never heard the real story about Garrick.

When I arrived, I learned of stories of Charlie's previous partner, Michael Hirschfeld—and the story of Hirschfeld's exit varies, depending on whose story you listened to. Michael's spirit was still there and people still talked about him daily. Besides Michael, you would hear stories of all the people who had worked there in the past: Bradley Mendelson, Ed Brock, and The Boys. The Boys, as they were referred to, consisted of Gary Alterman, Ben Fox, and Steve Ash. They had left Charlie to start their own firm that was called New Spectrum.

My area was great: in the research department with all the books stacked behind and in front of me. The desktop was 15 feet in length. They had one computer dedicated to the listings that I oversaw: all the available stores. My area was open and I was able to hear the ongoing chatter of the other brokers. I was thrilled to be there. This was my second shot to make it in the real estate industry.

There must have been 300 sheets that everyone received weekly, describing the stores that were available in New York City. No one was allowed to take the listings off the premises. The salespeople would get daily listings as well. There were 17,000 buildings in Manhattan and at any one time, we would have about 1,900 to 2,300 available stores listed.

This was a period before the commercial listing system company called CoStar got into the business. Garrick-Aug had the best listing system in the industry and that is what separated us from the other firms. When CoStar became popular, it leveled the playing field. But before them, we had all the available stores listed. Additionally, everyone had to contribute five new listings a month or you would get a deduction of one percent off your next commission. There were about 50 brokers, so every day the freshest listings were distributed to the salespeople. It was a great system guaranteeing you would have at least 250 new listings a month.

My job was to canvass Manhattan and put all the listings in the system of the available stores. I took the job seriously. I knew nothing about the contract that the property owner and the retailer used when a retailer leased a store, and that intimidated me. I also did not know how to negotiate a lease agreement. But be-damned, I promised myself I was going to know every available space, and once this six-month canvassing assignment (that paid $250 a week) was over, if a retailer or a restaurateur wanted a 1,000- or 10,000-square-foot space, I would be able to give them every option in the market.

I knew the retail sector of real estate was more emotional than investment sales. Investment sales was more about numbers. Accountants did especially well in that sector. I knew store leasing was more about retailers and their daily sales. The retailers were more interested in who their neighbors were and what type of pedestrian traffic was passing their store daily. Since I was a retailer and ran health clubs, I got the whole *Gestalt* of the equation and understood that the best retail location would be the one that fit the retailer's customer. I knew once a retailer fell in love with the location, I didn't have to worry about their potential sales. negotiating the deal or knowing specific clauses in the lease agreement. The rest would be easy, since who wants to break up a fine romance between the retailer and the location, when they fell in love?

From the first week, I made a copy of a street map from a Hagstrom map book and enlarged it to 30 inches in length. My objective was to learn the entire market and the valuation of each street. Every time I canvassed a street or avenue, I would return to the office and highlight the street canvassed. I wanted to know where I had canvassed, and which streets still needed to be scouted. I wanted to know the going price of a lease on a store on upper Broadway, compared to lower Broadway and all other streets and avenues. One of the previous canvassers was a fellow by the name of Robert Futterman. Robert was now a top manager at the firm that eventually opened his own firm many years later.

Soon, I learned that most of the past canvassers hardly walked all of Manhattan even once. I was determined to walk it several times—and in the next six-month period, I canvassed Manhattan three times. I was so persistent, I threw my back out and had to get a new pair of shoes with rubber sole cushions to ease the pain. I knew if my back didn't improve, it could have blown my chance of succeeding, so I was constantly saying a few prayers here and there to get better quickly.

All the managers noticed I had gumption. How couldn't they? I was inputting at least 10 new listings a day. Most of the previous canvassers were in their 20s and I was 31, which was considered old for a canvasser. All the managers were courting me to work for them and likewise, I was studying them to see whom I would like to work for.

One day Faith Hope Consolo came over to the canvassing area. She was a top manager and an important person in the firm. She had done many large deals, recently bringing Zara from Spain, Paul Smith from London, and Matsuda from Japan, Alain Mikli from Paris. She was a pretty woman with reddish or strawberry blonde hair, which was coiffed like Catherine Deneuve's, never a hair out of place. It was always shiny. She looked as though her hair stylist had just left. Her skin was translucent, not a mark on it except a well positioned natural beauty mark on her cheek and her eyes were dark brown. She constantly pushed her hair back with her left hand and amazingly, it would fall back into place. She dressed impeccably, wearing important-looking and elegant jewelry. Her presence was similar to that of Miranda Priestly from *The Devil Wears Prada*. She was full-figured, and you knew when this woman entered a room she was powerful.

She said, "What is your name?" I said, "Joe Aquino."

She said "You're *Italiannnnn*?"

She immediately added; "Thank God we have another Italian here. These Jewish guys are still fighting the Six Day War." Most of the salespeople surrounding us were Jewish and they all laughed. "Where are you from?"

"Brooklyn."

"Where in Brooklyn?"

I told her some of the different neighborhoods I had lived in. We continued to talk. She was sitting next to me now. No one else could hear us.

She said, "Tell me about your family!" I replied that my dad had been a longshoreman and that he died when I was 12 and my mom had died when I was 22 and I had one sister.

I said, "How about you?"

"My father died when I was two," she told me, "my mom died when I was 12 and I was raised by my grandmother who died when I was 21. I am an only child, "she paused.

Immediately, my heart went out to Faith. I knew the pain of losing my folks at an early age and I could only imagine what she went through losing hers and she had no siblings. From then on, we had a bond, and I had a new friend in the firm. Every day, she would pass me notes to canvas for her and I would bring her the correct info within 30 to 60 minutes. She once told me that the other canvassers would take days. Some of the canvassers would never come back with any information.

One day, Faith overheard that I was taking the new canvasser out to lunch on a Saturday afternoon, in Soho since I was in the fifth month of my six month tenure. His name was Brian Sim. I am still friends with him up until today. She said, "Would you mind hanging a for-rent sign for me?" I told her it would be my pleasure.

That Saturday, I took Brian to a restaurant in Soho located on West Broadway called I Tre Merli, which means "three crows" in Italian. The restaurant was operated by an Italian family that owned a vine-yard back in Italy. The ceiling was high, with fans circulating the hot summer air. One wall, which was the complete length of the restau-rant, was brick and along its ledge stood bottles of their wine.

After lunch with Brian, I walked over to the store on West Broadway to hang the sign. As I was securing the sign, someone knocked on the window. I opened it and said, "Can I help you?" They asked if the store was for rent." and I said, "Yes, please come in."

I must admit I was as nervous as heck, not ever having shown a store before. I started walking this gentleman through the premises like I was back at the health club. I started calling out the areas, saying, this is the dressing room, this is the basement, this is where the boiler room area is, and when I went back upstairs, I announced, "Oh, yeah, and this is the selling area," in case he missed it.

I asked him what he sold and he said, "Spanish-made shearling coats." When I was a teenager, I used to work for Shepherd's Hut selling shearling coats, so right away we had something in common—lucky me. He asked the price, and I realized I didn't have it—but sure enough, I got his business card and I gave him my information and promised him that on Monday he would have the full details.

On Monday, I immediately told Faith of my good fortune. She took the card and said, "I will call him now." She walked over to my desk later to tell me that he was making an offer. I could not believe it. Well, maybe I could believe it, because I knew my luck was changing.

Faith submitted the offer to the property owner, whose name was Joseph Gardner. He called Faith up and said, "Orchard Street?"

Faith said, "Yes Orchard Street, that is where his store is now," aware that the street was known to be a low-rent district. I even knew that Orchard Street had that reputation, because as a youth, I had bought a leather jacket there only to arrive home to learn it was "pleather." Which is plastic leather.

By now, Soho was a chic neighborhood that only attracted high-end stores. Joe, the property owner, wasn't sure this would be the right tenant for his store. Faith went on to tell him, "Mishon told me his coats are very expensive. They average $2,000 to $3,000 and his clientele is wealthy Jewish ladies that shop on Sunday."

Joe said, "Okay, go and see his store, and if you like it, I will do the deal with him."

Faith went to visit the store and she loved it. She called Joe on return to the office and reported her findings. Joe then countered the offer. Faith immediately called Mishon and he said he would get back to her the following day, that he had to discuss it with his wife. The next day he called Faith and said that he accepted the offer and Faith immediately asked him to send her his financials—and the call ended.

Bad financials can kill a deal, but sure enough, Mr. Mishon had good ones. Joseph Gardner was a certified public accountant and if Joe accepted them, then you know that the proposed tenant had a good balance sheet.

After about a month Faith closed the deal, the year is 1989. Shortly thereafter, I received my first check from the deal, in the amount of $6,000. In that period of my life that was a lot of money. When I sold the shopping center, I only walked away with $15,000 and now I made this deal in a much quicker time and this was only one of two installments. Once the store opened, I would get another $6,000, for a total of $12,000.

That evening, Faith invited me to a meeting with her. She was pleased we had closed the deal. We were sitting in the back of a car service limousine, heading downtown.

Faith asked, "Did you receive the check?"

I said, "Yes."

She looked over and said, "What's wrong? You look upset."

I felt a tear run down my cheek—grateful, overwhelmed.

"You don't know what it took for me to get here," I said quietly.

By then, Faith knew parts of my story—we were talking every day. She nodded, understanding. With confidence and warmth, she said, "This is just the beginning. We're going to do a lot more deals together."

During this period, I started listening to Anthony Robbins' cassettes on his theory on how to succeed.

When I was working at the Business School, I was taking the subway back and forth to work. I loved business books and biographies too. One of my favorites was *Barbarians to Bureaucrats* by Lawrence M. Miller, about a business life cycle. The book taught me how to read a company and where it was in its business cycle. For example, in the "barbarian" stage, you have a guy like Ray Kroc who pulled himself up by his bootstraps and formed McDonalds in his late 50s. Then at some point a guy like that would retire or pass away and the company would go into the hands of attorneys and accountants—and they would run the show. This is called the bureaucratic and administrative stage and that is usually when a company starts to falter. The sales go south. Then, ideally, someone comes on the scene like Lee Iacocca, who took Chrysler out of bankruptcy and brought them back to life and into the number one spot again. This book helped me in my real estate career, when I worked with retailers and real estate families, because it helped me recognize whom I was dealing with and at what cycle the company is presently in—and how to advise them.

Another book I read and recommend is *Behind the Golden Arches*, by James Love, one of the better books written about Ray Kroc, the McDonald brothers and McDonald's Corporation. Ray's legacy was to promise consistency in the food—wherever there was a McDonald's in the world. He used to perpetrate "potato raids" on his vendors at 4:00 in the morning, and if he found the potatoes buried underground (which was how they were traditionally stored, rather than refrigerated at the company-specified temperature), he would terminate their contract on the spot. Ray was my hero. Aspiring to be Ray, I learned what it took to be a great manager, since I was one for eight years running health clubs.

I also read books about Harold Geneen, who headed the ITT Corporation. He always wanted his managers to put their departments' major problems on the first page of the report in red, and not bury them in the rear. I also read stories about Sony, Wang and NBC.

Reading about Henry Kissinger was exceptional too. He was so smart and a great diplomat. Each of these books had a special message and lesson for me.

Six months flew by and I was about finished with the canvassing position job. Soon I would be coming off the salary of $250 a week. I was really feeling good about myself and then Charlie sat me down in his office. He announced to me that he was moving me to the boroughs.

"You are going to help Peter."

Peter was the manager of the outer boroughs: Queens, Brooklyn, Staten Island, and the Bronx. I was shocked. I immediately said, "No, I am not doing that!"

"Charlie, I just walked Manhattan three times; I know Manhattan like the back of my hand. Why would you send me to the boroughs?"

"Peter needs you."

I wasn't particularly fond of Peter. Nothing personal against him, but we had never had a single conversation in six months. Peter always walked past me as though I wasn't there.

I told Charlie, "I cannot do it. My car is old and breaks down frequently and you cannot afford to fix my car every week." Then I dropped the gauntlet: "Anyway, Faith and I decided I am going on her team."

Charlie said, "No one tells me what to do in my company."

I repeated that I simply was not going to the boroughs, and I invited Charlie to talk to Faith about it.

I went back to my desk and I stayed quiet. I just sat it out. I managed to tell Faith what transpired and Faith said she would talk to Charlie. I knew Charlie wanted to do what Steve did when I was back at Jack Lanne. He wanted me to go to a place I knew was wrong.

Lesson learned: When you know you're right, just stand your ground.

Every manager was flirting with me to be on their team. When I was unemployed, I had read a few passages from the Bible and one passage always stood out, "Choose the path with the most heart." I knew Faith would give me a fair shake; I wasn't sure about the other managers. A few days went by and finally, Faith came over to me and said, "Okay, Charlie agreed."

Faith had about eight people on her team, half of whom were called

Garrick Aug Worldwide. Their jobs were to bring tenants in from around the globe. The other half were just working on the Manhattan local market. Faith had salespeople who were from France, Italy, and England, and another who was Spanish, but not from Spain. One of my jobs was to canvas for Faith's international brokers' customers. She made me an offer to canvas for her salespersons and in return for 10 percent of the deal, and I happily said yes.

I worked nicely with her team, finding spaces for their customers over the next year. One week, I canvassed every retailer on Madison Avenue, asking if they would sell their lease. No one had done this before and when I showed Faith the results, you would have thought I was giving her a bar of gold. We had all the listings and then some. The first deal I did for her group was Maud Frizon, a French designer shoe brand. I found them a space at 829 Madison Avenue. The second was CP Company, a major Italian brand that was part of the GFT Group. Rita Anichini, who headed Faith's team in Italy, brought her the CP Company. Faith asked me to find them a space in the Flatiron District and within a week, I uncovered an off-the-market space in the Flatiron Building. That's that famous triangular-shaped building on Fifth Avenue and 23rd Street. The space I uncovered was the corner. Astra Trading was the tenant and the windows were darkened with red paint. They were a toy wholesaler, so they didn't need to have clear visible windows. The Flatiron District was the new hot and trendy area. The vice president of CP Company called his boss to say the corner was available: a space shaped like a narrow slice of cake. The owner of GFT said, "The Flatiron Building? I am an architect by trade; I wrote my thesis on that property. Make the deal." We did.

When CP Company opened, the parent company threw a huge party with one of those Hollywood searchlights scouring the sky outside of the store. This was the heyday of fashion when there was no budget for getting your name out there. Champagne at the parties flowed endlessly and the guest list was a *Who's Who*. Paul Smith, to whom Faith had leased a store a few blocks down on Fifth Avenue, attended. He flew in from London to be present.

By now, our French salesperson, Chantal Eisenger, had moved to Paris. Charlie paid for her *pied à terre* there. Faith and Charlie made a good team and they were both ahead of their time in the globalization of retail. Charlie supported all of Faith's travel to Europe—which amounted to a lot.

My third deal was Goldpfeil, a German company that made leather goods. They were one of the first companies to dye their goods in primary colors. Their handbags were bright red, blue, yellow, and green. We located them at 711 Fifth Avenue at the corner of 55th Street. They had fallen in love with this corner, which also housed Nat Sherman. That was another off-the-market space I brought to Faith's team. I remember, she told me to call the building when we walked by the property. There was a store in the middle of the building called Kimbe Optics, that she felt didn't belong there. When I called the broker, I began the conversation by saying, "I know you have a store at 711 Fifth Avenue. What are the details of Kimbe Optics?"

To my surprise, he replied, "No, it's not Kimbe Optics, it's the corner, Nat Sherman, that is becoming available." I had totally bluffed him. I knew now I was going to get the details to the corner, which was even better. I went back to tell Faith and she couldn't believe it. We had the details of the best corner on Fifth Avenue to present to Goldpfeil.

Coca-Cola owned the building. Faith would have to deal with the executives in Atlanta, where Coke was headquartered. That deal took about six to eight weeks to complete. After our initial tour of the premises with the President of Goldpfeil, Ingo Kaiser, he sent Faith a half a dozen bags with his beautiful company brochure to present to the executive board at Coke. The executives loved the product and that was half the battle; the other half was the rent and the tenant's financials.

The rent back then was $1,500 per square foot. Fifth Avenue always had the highest rent, not only in New York City, but in the entire United States. The deal got struck at the asking price and Goldpfeil built a beautiful store.

In addition to finding the off-the-market space, I was the one who got the initial meeting with Goldpfeil. I always felt there were three balls to a deal. One ball is the tenant. You cannot do a deal without a tenant. The second ball is the space. If you have no space, there is not a store in which to set up shop. The third ball is the marketplace. There are outer forces that try to kill your deal. One of these outer forces is time. The longer a deal is out, the higher the chances it can get squashed by your competition. To make the deal, you must press the three balls together swiftly, and then to fuse them into one, in order to make the deal before someone tries to kill it. We had the tenant, we had the space, but if Faith didn't go in there and fuse the property owner to the deal, we had nothing.

Once the deal was completed, Faith gave me a higher share of the split for getting the tenant to work with us along with finding the space. My commission for this transaction was $90,000—and for 1990, that was spectacular.

Faith treated me well from the start. When we handled the store on West Broadway for the shearling coat company, for example, she shared the commission equally.

Lesson learned, Remember the three balls.

Before e-mails and e-blasts, we did mailings with the U.S. Post office. We would do a 20,000-piece mailing as though it was nothing. Charlie happily supplied the postage. Roy Salmon was our in-house mail guy, and he did a terrific job getting it out on a timely basis. We would do mailings on all the properties for which we were the exclusive agents. Generally, no one would do follow-up calls, but I did. I called all the retailers on the mailings and soon found out everyone's requirements. I knew who wanted a new store; who wanted to get out of an old store. This was all prior to artificial intelligence. If you were willing to do the work, you could easily get to the head of the class. You just had to have the desire and the follow through.

Things were going well, over weeks, then over months, then over years.

We were doing all the work for Cosmetics Plus, Innovation Luggage, Au Bon Pain, and were working for Zara, but they had not found their footing yet. They weren't sure America was the right place for them. We even got a call that they were considering leaving their only location in the United States that Faith made prior to my arrival: at 750 Lexington Avenue, across from Bloomingdale's. They even hired us to dispose of that space and thank goodness, there were no bidders. They had a large 15,000-square-foot selling basement that no one knew how to use. The big-box stores still had not arrived in Manhattan. I met a young lady once on a plane and she said she would never wear Zara clothing. I asked why. She said their sizing was messed up. She said the only size that fit her was a 14 and she was a size 7. She added, "I am not going to a party and put my jacket on the sofa with a size 14 on the collar." I immediately informed Zara and they said they were aware of the problem and they were fixing it. Faith even did a Today's Man store with Fern Glanzrock and Robert Futterman at 529 Fifth Avenue, where Larry Silverstein was the property owner. That store was the start of the big-box craze, having 30,000 square feet and only selling men's clothing.

VII. THE TIMES SQUARE/42ND STREET PROJECT

In 1991 we got a call from the Urban Development Corporation, (UDC), a New York State agency, to assist them with the redevelopment of Times Square, which consisted of the block of 42nd Street between Seventh and Eighth Avenues. This was the block that has the highest concentration of theatres of anywhere in the world: nine (9) in all.

We were sitting in with Rebecca Robertson, the president of the 42nd Street Development Project, and her team. She rolled out the plan of the street showing the placement of all the buildings to scale. She said, "Faith and Joe, the State of New York owns half the block, and the other half is a red-light district. Do you think we can have a family center on one side and leave the other half the way it is?" Faith and I looked at her as though she weren't serious and we all laughed. The street had pimps, prostitutes and drug dealers all surrounding the movie theaters that mainly showed pornography. We knew that was impossible, but I guess she had to ask. She said, "I didn't think so."

Robertson went on to tell us that she was interviewing companies to assist them in raising $150 million dollars to complete their condemnation of the block. Condemnation is a police action force that the State uses to buy back the properties from property owners for the betterment of the community. Everyone sitting at the table felt there would be no resistance against this cause from the various community boards, which had a huge say as to what happened in the day-to-day life of the city.

I knew we didn't have a marketing department that could muster up the company's information that we needed for us to get the assignment. Nevertheless, I knew Garrick-Aug had the experience to win the assignment: more than 20 years as leaders in store leasing in Manhattan. I went to Charlie and told him he had to get all his managers to give us a list of their top 15 deals that they had done over the past 10 years.

I compiled a book of more than 300 transactions and we sent it to Rebecca Robertson with a cover letter about our company, along with a retail plan that would take the street from grit to glory. Rebecca called a few days later and told Faith she liked what she read and wanted to meet us again.

Faith and I were working with a man named Lee Philips who did quantitative, qualitative reports. He was brilliant at doing case studies of an area. Shopping mall developers would hire Lee to do the analysis, prior to their decision to build a million-square-foot mall. Developers would also use Lee's studies to secure financing. We brought Lee into the next meeting and he told Rebecca he would like to do a Focus Group to get the views and recommendations of all the present store and restaurant owners, other groups, and everyday consumers. She loved the idea. Lee also told her he wanted to do an intercept study to ask tourists and locals who walked Times Square their thoughts by asking them 10 stock questions. Rebecca loved that idea too. She recognized this was exactly what the project needed to take through the public process to get control of the block.

We were all on the same page and a week later, Rebecca hired us. Everyone in the city wanted to see the State make Times Square safe and bring in a family theme that also included an entertainment element.

In addition to formulating our retail plan (with the help of Lee's research studies), we were part of an All-Star team of real estate professionals. We had the famed architect, Robert A.M. Stern, who was responsible for the exteriors and a new architect, David Rockwell, who was responsible for the interiors of the theaters. David was also a student of Stern's in his architecture school. Rockwell eventually became as famous as Robert, designing all the Planet Hollywood theme restaurants. Both looked at the viability of the theatres and made recommendations for the retail uses. In addition to the architects, construction, engineers and the retail consultants, the team had sign and lighting consultants. Rebecca wanted to keep the character of Times Square bold. Faith and I would look at their recommendations and give our critique.

VIII. TRAVELING WITH FAITH CONSOLO

Faith and I went to visit outdoor centers in other states to get ideas to bring back to 42nd Street. We visited the new CocoWalk in Coconut Grove in Miami. It was shaped like a horseshoe and had two levels. It was an open-air center and most of the restaurants were on the second level. We liked it very much.

From there we flew to Horton Plaza in San Diego. We stayed at the Grand Hotel in the center of town. San Diego was a little sleepy for me, but Horton Plaza was nice. It was larger than CocoWalk, but had the same two-level horseshoe configuration, with lots of restaurants and national retailers.

We went to visit the Hotel Del Coronado and had lunch there, where they had filmed the famous movie *Some Like It Hot*, with Marilyn Monroe, Tony Curtis and Jack Lemmon.

On Friday, Faith announced that we were going to ride 60 miles north on the coast and we were going to visit every shopping mall on the return. That Friday morning, the start of Labor Day weekend, we set out on our journey. We spent the next eight hours trudging through every mall. After a while, they all started to look alike. Faith had incredible stamina and finally on the seventh one, I said, "Let me take a seat and you can walk around." By this time, I had three shopping bags of goods we had purchased along the way. On her return, she found me sleeping sitting up. I never had a problem sleeping, often boasting I could sleep on a bed of nails.

Faith told me there was an elderly lady sitting next to me and she told Faith, "Don't worry, I've been watching him, and he's okay." Faith thanked her. I was Faith's junior by 10 years and she often joked with me about my inability to keep up with her—and she was right.

Back on the highway, I couldn't wait to get to the hotel to take a shower and get ready for dinner. Faith said, "Ralph Lauren just opened a store in Tijuana," and she wanted to see it.

"Tijuana? Are you serious?"

"Come on, we're here, let's go." I knew I couldn't win.

We had about another hour's drive and finally we reached the border. Faith was acting like a high school girl; she couldn't wait to get out of the car. As I was parking, Faith already had her hand on the car door.

I said, "Where are you going?"

"Tijuana, why?"

"Not with that jewelry on."

She had expensive gold bracelets and jewelry on both wrists; one had rubies. Her fingers were bejeweled with rings and she wore a beautiful pearl necklace inlaid with gold around her neck. In her left hand was the original Motorola flip phone that I had got her that was as big as a grenade with its antenna—and let's not forget that she had her Chanel bag over her shoulder.

I said, "Put all that jewelry away before they chop your hands off or kidnap us."

Can you imagine, our kidnappers calling up Charlie for a million-dollar ransom and him telling them, 'Sorry, I don't have the money, you can keep them"?

Faith refused to leave the jewelry in the glove compartment, so she put all the jewelry and the phone into her bag. We now started to walk to the border.

We were about one hundred feet from walking over the border—in a line that was moving slowly. Suddenly, about 100 Mexicans at once broke the border at the checkpoint and started running around the cars and walkways that were lined up on the United States side. As they ran past us, I shielded Faith against the wall like the bodyguard from the movie of the same name. They were running fast and furious adjacent to us, striking me with their elbows, knees and feet. We both turned after we realized they were gone, and all we could see in the distance were police chasing them down the highway both by foot and by car with sirens and twirling lights. The overall effect was like a torrential rainstorm that left as quickly as it had come.

I looked Faith directly in the eye and said, "Did you have enough? Can we go back to our hotel?"

"No, I want to go see the Ralph Lauren store."

Faith was fearless.

As soon as we went over the border, you knew you were no longer in Kansas anymore. Now we had to find a cab. The cab we got wasn't like the ones we had in Manhattan: it was a low rider like the one that Freddie Prinze described in his comedy routine. A low rider is a car with little or no shocks and the car's bottom is practically touching the street. It even had a bobblehead doll on the back window.

It was about 6:30 pm on a Friday evening, on the Labor Day weekend. We were driving slowly toward the Ralph Lauren store. I knew it would be dark soon. The buildings were two stories, as in CocoWalk and Horton Plaza, but this was not a planned themed development. We were in a town with mostly bars and restaurants, where it appeared that a lot of the locals had already had their fill of beer, rum, and tequila. People were hanging out of the second-floor terraces singing and whistling. The whistling followed us as we crawled down the street in our car. I felt as though we had been identified by our kidnappers and they were informing each other that they had found their catch for the day.

Not to mention, our driver didn't speak much English. I felt as though I was in a *Twilight Zone* movie. The driver saw I was upset as I kept talking and asking questions and he wasn't responding. Finally he stopped the car at a corner by a traffic light and got out. He returned a few minutes later with a man who spoke perfect English and asked us where we wanted to go. He passed this information to our driver, and we were back on our way.

Shortly thereafter, our driver turned off the main street and stopped in the middle of the block. This was not the main road and I was concerned, thinking that we were going to be ambushed. There was a house that looked like the one Archie Bunker had lived in, in Ozone Park, Queens in the sitcom *All In The Family*: a detached house with a small garden and a walkway. He pointed to it and sure enough, there was a small sign that read, "Ralph Lauren." There was no one else on the block except the three of us. Even though my driver didn't speak English, I was not sure I wanted to part with him, because who knew how or when we would find another cab. I asked Faith if we should keep him, and she said, "Don't be ridiculous, let him go."

We walked up to the store and entered it, and immediately, I felt safe, since every sign in the store was in English. I treated the store as though it were the U.S. Embassy.

It was a store of only about 600 square feet and as I started to feel safe, then I looked out the window to see a brick wall with red painted letters about fifty feet wide which read, "Live Transexual Shows Every 30 Minutes." I said to myself, "Okay, that's great," recalling a scene that took place in *The Godfather Part 2*, where Freddie took Michael and colleagues to a nightclub in Cuba and they saw a sex show.

Faith now wanted to leave and walk the town—which meant leaving our safety.

I said, "Oh no, I am not walking around. Let's get another cab and he will drive through the town." She agreed, knowing there was no negotiating this time.

In our next cab we told the driver (who had assured us that he spoke English) that we wanted to see all the retail in town. The driver stopped at every bar and waited.

After the fifth stop, I said, "What are we doing? We want to see retail, the stores."

"Oh, I thought you wanted to go to all the bars."

He admitted that there really was no retail in Tijuana, and kept driving. Soon, I saw that he was right: there was no retail to speak of. I thought, "That's good. Now we can get out of Tijuana." I turned to Faith and said, "Okay, have you seen enough? Can we go back to the hotel?"

She said, "Okay, let's go back"

I asked the driver to take us to the border. Suddenly, he became chatty, telling us that we should stay overnight and that he knew of a place that had running water, a TV and a telephone. I said, "Oh no." I envisioned that he was going to drive us somewhere in the mountains and make that call to Charlie for the ransom money. Firmly, I said to him, "No, take us to the border, now."

"Are you sure? It's a lovely place."

Firmly, I repeated, "No, we want the border, now!"

We made it to the U.S. and to our hotel. When we returned to the office we told the other team members of our journey—not in detail, but we did tell them that we went to Tijuana. Two weeks later, another one of our team members was in Southern California and decided to take his wife and two children to see Tijuana. Our colleague was a little frugal that day and decided to save on the parking lot fee. He parked his rental car on the street. On his return at the end of the day when there was no more sun, he saw that his car had been stolen. He had to contact the police and the car rental company. His family didn't get back to their hotel till midnight that evening.

Being a Brooklyn boy, you know when to sense danger. Lesson learned: Trust your instincts.

IX. BACK IN TIMES SQUARE

For the next few months, Faith and I visited the nine (9) Times Square theatres in their vacant state and put together a retail plan that New York State liked and envisioned putting into play. The report named museums such as Madame Tussaud's, La Cage aux Folles, a jazz club, corporate sponsors taking over some of the theaters, large restaurants, entertainment users and many other types of fun retail.

Today it appears to be a no brainer, but back then many people thought it was impossible, since most of the small property owners were only interested in getting top dollar by leasing their spaces to porn-related uses. During this period Times Square was dangerous, and what New York State was doing was long overdue.

The day came when a public hearing had to review what we were proposing. This was an important day because the plan could have received resistance. The most amazing thing happened. The plan got approved on the first round, which is seldom heard of. There is always one group in the city that gives resistance, but this time everyone supported our plan. It was officially approved a few weeks later.

By the winter the plan was approved, and the State did what they had planned: They took control of the buildings they did not own. The State now had control of the entire block and all the theaters and stores were shut down and boarded up for safekeeping.

At the first snowfall, the pimps, prostitutes, drug dealers, and porn hustlers left. Not one person was standing in front of the theatres or stores anymore. A few days later, another snowfall came and still no one was standing on the streets. Soon spring was on the horizon. We were convinced that when spring arrived, our "friends" would return. But to our disbelief, not one of them came back. Everyone on our team felt relieved.

The State officials knew they were not in the development business, so for the next part of the plan they decided to divide up the block among experienced developers. Within nine months, in came Forest City Ratner, then Durst, and Tishman— maybe not in that order, but these were the players ready to build and construct.

Robert A.M. Stern was on the Disney board of directors and had designed the Dolphin Hotel in Florida for them. As soon as the State had control, he brought in Michael Eisner, the CEO from Disney, to view all the theaters on the street. Michael liked the New Amsterdam theatre and shortly thereafter secured it for Disney. This is where he eventually hosted *The Lion King* and other shows such as *Aladdin & Beauty and the Beast*.

Once the State had divided up 42nd Street, we got a call by Forest City Ratner. Bruce Ratner headed up the east coast market for his family that was based out of Cleveland.

Faith and I got to do our dog and pony show. This time it was in front of Bruce. We were already the retail consultants for the street, so our confidence level was at an all-time high. From Bruce's conversation, I recognized that he was going out to all the brokers asking them to make six of their best calls for the project.

Seeing the opportunity, I said, "Bruce, it appears you're talking to all the brokers, asking them to reach out to some of their tenants. Faith and I can go back to the office and call five or six people, or we can go back and reach out to 5,000 of our customers."

Then I went in for the close. "Do you want us to go back to the office and contact five or six companies or reach out to 5,000?" I then kept quiet, because the first person who speaks loses, remember my earlier lesson? He answered, "Five thousand." Immediately, Faith chimed in, closed her folder and said, "Okay, Bruce, let us go back to the office and we will send you an agreement."

We did exactly that and after he signed, we had a 200-foot-wide sign affixed to the Eighth Avenue side of the Ratner project. When anyone walked out of the Port Authority Bus Terminal, they immediately saw the verbiage that 100,000 square feet was available, along with the names of Faith Hope Consolo and Joseph Aquino as the exclusive leasing agents.

Now Faith and I were the experts of Times Square. We got a call to represent the retail at 1633 Broadway. We pitched the owners and won that assignment too. We were now representing the Paramount Group, a German property owner that also owned *Spiegel catalogue*. This was the building where John Kennedy Jr., had offices for his magazine, *George*. Once the project started, I used to see John, Jr., all the time rollerblading to work. He was as handsome in person as he was in photos.

In addition to handling their retail space, they also hired us to be the retail consultants for the redesign of their plaza. We helped them select an architectural team: Paul Rosen and Anthony Johnson of Rosen and Johnson. The office building design was black glass and steel with an unexciting plaza area. Paul and Anthony did a terrific job of bringing the plaza up to date with proper lighting, new stone plaza area, and other features. The space had two large wells and they did a nice job with the sign plan, popping out the storefronts. While they were redesigning the plaza area, Faith and I managed to secure several tenants.

We did a 35,000-square-foot Equinox deal that Robert Futterman from our company brought us. The Mars 2112 theme restaurant deal was another 35,000-square-foot transaction. Inside the elevator cab was designed to look like the inside of a spaceship and when you appeared to have blasted off, you ended up inside the restaurant downstairs, where you thought you were on the surface of Mars. It was one of the first of many theme restaurants Manhattan would attract. We also did a fast-food restaurant called Così, which had a wood burning brick oven warming up the bread to the sandwiches while the customer watched on. Robert Kunikoff from our office represented Così, while Faith and I represented the property owner, Paramount.

Across the street, Robert Kunikoff scored another deal. He landed Lundy's Restaurant, from Sheepshead Bay, Brooklyn. Lundy's was a world-renowned 100-year-old fish restaurant. They were located next door to the Winter Garden Theater, where the long-running musical *Cats*, by Andrew Lloyd Webber, was playing. This area was known as Times Square North. We were part of building up this area too, just as the southern portion of 42nd Street was blossoming. Caroline's Comedy Club opened shortly thereafter, one block away on Broadway between 49th and 50th Streets.

Now New York City was firing on all cylinders. Faith and I were pleased with the results of our contribution to Times Square. Bruce Ratner performed a feat of the century: he moved the Empire Movie Theatre on an improvised train track, from one part of the project to the other. The distance was about 170 feet, and it took an entire day to inch it along.

During our exclusive period Faith and I did several deals. Robert Greenstone from our office brought us Applebee's restaurant for 12,000 square feet mainly on the second floor and then we did an international newsstand and a 25,000 square foot Just for Feet store that mainly sold sneakers that Leslie Mayer brought us from Beverly Hills where she is from.

Within one year of getting approval to complete the condemnation to take back the properties of 42nd Street, the City of New York was bragging that crime in Times Square for the past 12 months went down by 72 percent. That was incredible, and everyone involved in the project was pleased. The red-light district of 42nd Street was no more.

CHAPTER X. CARTIER/FIFTH AVENUE

Shortly thereafter, Faith got a call from Cartier. The CEO, Simon Critchel, was whispering into the phone. He explained that Cartier was coming off a long-term lease that was about 70 to 75 years old, and 10 years prior Cartier had sued the landlord—the Onassis Foundation—for lack of services because the property was not being heated adequately. Cartier took the landlord to court and won, but now the property owner was not talking to them and it was time to renew.

Faith said she had thought Cartier owned the building. Critchel replied, "Yes, the story goes, Cartier exchanged pearls for the property, but the Onassis Foundation is the true owner. Now we need to get talking to them or we are going to lose this location."

Our assignment was, first to open a dialogue with the property owner and get a renewal, or

secondly – to move them. Sounds simple, right?

For the next four months Faith and I, and the Cartier team, were feverishly negotiating in good faith, no pun intended. We would attend meetings at the Cartier mansion and hear jokes about the people from the other country, and we would always laugh. The French had their Greek jokes, and the Greeks their share of French jokes. You felt like you were at a European soccer match final, with everyone wearing their team shirts.

During all these negotiations, I was showing Cartier other spaces in the marketplace, which couldn't compare what they had. How do you replace their location in a beautiful mansion on the best corner of Fifth Avenue and 52nd Street?

This was a period of theme stores. Other property owners were securing companies like Warner Brothers which displayed Superman on top of their elevator, visible from the street, going up and down like he was naturally flying. When the elevator went up, so did Superman. It was catchy and these were the types of tenants that were looking for key locations on Fifth Avenue. Faith got wind that another theme company was talking to the property owner and that's when Faith told the executive board if they did not fly to Athens to meet the Onassis Board directly and stop this going back and forth, to just start packing their boxes now. Simon agreed.

The trip was scheduled for three weeks from the day Faith made her request, and Faith had a personal trainer exercising her every day. We took her off all the dairy products and increased her water intake. This was a big moment in her career, and she wanted to be in the best shape when she landed. Her personal trainer increased her work out and every night she met him for ninety minutes to be trained military style, doing full runs, squats, lunges, hand weights, with no scheduled breaks. I imagined when Faith got off the plane she would be tearing the yellow pages telephone apart with her bare hands. She told me later that when the plane touched down on the tarmac, the limousine was waiting to whisk her away. She said her feet never touched the ground.

That evening, everyone dined with the Foundation, and Cartier's CFO started negotiating at the dinner table. Faith gave him a shot in the ribs with her elbow. He whispered, what was that for? She said in Greece, they never talk business while eating. There will be a time when we talk business, but it will not be tonight. He understood, and they continued to enjoy their meal.

Faith said the dining room was facing the Parthenon, which is a temple on the Athenian Acropolis dedicated to the goddess Athena. She said the view was breathtaking. Faith told me it took several days to negotiate, along with many great meals, but at the end they all hugged and kissed each other on both cheeks as Europeans do, and the deal was sealed.

On the way back Faith missed her plane and took another. The plane she missed crashed, while making a landing at Kennedy Airport. She was traveling with Ralph Destino who was the Chairman of Cartier at the time. Both their lives were spared.

XI. BRANDING

For as long as I knew Faith, she published a Manhattan Report: a quarterly report on the state of the Manhattan marketplace, reporting on all the new store and restaurant openings and other important events. She would mail it out, and other brokers would use it as theirs. Faith had a notepad that measured about three by three inches. It was cute and it had her first name scripted clearly on the top in red. She would give her staff and others to-do notes or requests on this pad. One day I was hanging over her secretaries' desk and I took the Faith notepad and in front of her name I wrote the word, "The" and after her name I wrote "Report." Thus was born The Faith Report. I walked into her office to show her what I had done, and we both smiled. We both knew the Manhattan Report would be used no longer.

Our ad agent, Andrew Miller of Miller Advertising, took the name and went even further. We advertised all the time, and our ads were always next to other commercial brokers like Edward S. Gordon (which eventually became CBRE) and Cushman & Wakefield. One day Andrew placed the header, "You Need Faith!" across the top of our ad. That said it all. Above that line, in smaller letters, it said, "To Find the Best Retail." So there we were. The market loved it. Overnight, with my and Andrew's help, Faith had branded herself.

During this period, the early 1990s, the internet came into play, and no one could imagine the power it would have. Nevertheless, we realized it was a new media venue and we wanted to be part of it. I quickly recognized that the address was important, and I came up with www. faith-consolo.com. I hoped people would remember to include the dash between her names, or they would never get to her site. I thought, though, that omitting the hyphen would have taken away from her name. The hyphen worked perfectly.

We also had to design the website, and I came up with a few story boards. By now Faith and her team were doing all these deals with name tenants from all around the world. I was involved in most of them since I canvassed for her team members. I envisioned an opening page, where the names of the tenants would slide left to right, and from right to left would slide the cities from around the world. They would join together—and then, "To Find The Best" would slide from the left to right and "You Need Faith" would slide from the right to left. At the end, "To Find The Best Retail Space, You Need Faith" would appear in the middle and then all the tenants and city names would disappear. It was genius.

Early on, we selected a light pink as the main color, because it was both feminine and strong. From the beginning we started displaying our properties within the site, and Faith's articles. We were the first ones to have a personal website. Now everyone has one. Our company, Garrick Aug, didn't have one then, and still didn't till years later. I built a masterpiece—but the concept didn't catch on immediately. Virtually no other company or team was using a website. When we listed a property, we would list the names of the neighboring merchants (like Jimmy Choo, or Ferragamo) and we used to get email inquiries, asking where we could buy Jimmy Choo shoes? I realized that we weren't capturing our customer, but we kept it going and built the best site in the industry. Faith said, "Should we stop using it?" I said, "No, it will catch on, it hasn't found our audience yet." meaning our customers.

Today, it's common to see every company and broker's branding. One of the first branding successes was Barbara Corcoran and her namesake firm; another was the TV series *Million Dollar Listing*. However, early on, hardly any brokers did their individual marketing. They depended solely on the company. In fact, companies at first were not welcoming to the brokers doing their own branding. They feared it. Now they expect it.

Now Faith had The Faith Report; the slogan, "To Find the Best Retail Space, You Need Faith"; and her own website, www.faith-consolo.com. The press and landlords loved it, and we promoted these marketing tools all around the world.

Lesson learned; Find a way to separate yourself from the herd and marketplace.

XII. LAS VEGAS/LOS ANGELES

For years, Faith and I attended the International Conference of Shopping Centers (ICSC), held annually in Las Vegas. The event took place every May, right before the weekend of Memorial Day. Garrick Aug always had a splendid booth, and Charlie would give Faith the main corner of the booth, where the major foot traffic was, to display our properties. During this period, we always had about 20 stores available, and our job was to get them leased. The show had some 25,000 attendees, so this was the place to do it.

We worked closely with Andrew at Miller Advertising to develop ad campaigns to get the properties leased. The "You Need Faith" ads went into all the trade publications. And whatever ad we designed would also be printed on the shopping bags that we would hand out. Every year we would have 5,000 bags delivered to the booth and I would personally hand them out, striking up conversations with the retailers. My eyesight used to be as sharp as an eagle's, and I could read an attendee's badge from a 10-foot distance. We also had Andrew make a cute cartoon video of a New York City taxi driving the streets of Manhattan and at the end of the commercial it would say, "To Find the Best Retail, You Need Faith!" That ad was displayed on all the monitors and since few companies participated in this marketing event, the TV ad ran continuously all day long.

I started going to Las Vegas in 1989 and over the years I saw it built to what it is today. The first hotel I stayed at was the Riviera, which on

99

a street map looked like it was adjacent to the Las Vegas Convention Center. The Riviera was old-school and you felt at any moment that you were going to see a member of the Rat Pack checking out of a room with a gal he had picked up the night before. The dominant color in the hotel lobby and the rooms was maroon, and everywhere you looked you would see smokey stained-glass mirrors with gold motifs.

The map was deceiving. The hotel was a one-mile walk to the Convention Center, and it was 95 degrees outside at 8:00 A.M. Most days the temperature by noon far exceeded 101 degrees. There is rarely a cloud in the sky in Las Vegas, so you get sunburned in no time. By the time I walked one mile, I was soaked. That was the last time I walked a street in Las Vegas. Afterwards, I would only travel by cab.

Steve Wynn finally built the Bellagio, which was filmed in the movie *Ocean's Eleven* with George Clooney and Brad Pitt. The Bellagio originally was the epicenter of the new Las Vegas. Wynn raised the bar, with regard to what Las Vegas would look like. All the rooms were beautifully designed, including the common areas and elevators. The entire lobby area where you checked in was a quarter the size of a football field. It had a ceiling of colorful huge blown stained-glass flowers from Murano. You saw brilliant, beautiful colors like soft pinks, light greens, faded yellows, tropic blues, and bright oranges. The restaurants were beautifully designed by famous architects and had five-star chefs. Then there were the famous fountains that greeted you when you entered the driveway which encompassed the entire front of the property. They were over 1,000 feet in length and fronted the Las Vegas Strip. They danced in four-minute cycles, soaring to 460 feet in height. In the evening they started every 30 minutes dancing to the music of Frank Sinatra. If you ever go to the Bellagio, insist you get a room fronting the Strip. They pipe the music into the rooms if you wish to listen.

Eventually the other hotels started to spring up like popcorn. The Paris, a French theme hotel, was built directly across the street from the Bellagio. Its entranceway greeted you with a smaller scaled model, about one third in size of the Eiffel Tower and the Arc de Triomphe.

Down the Strip, you can visit the Venetian Hotel, which has a replica of the canals in Venice—with your own gondola and gondolier singing Italian songs to you and your colleagues.

Then there were the Forum Shops at Caesars Palace, with its Roman-themed columns and storefronts and the ceiling that changes from day to night. They also have grand fountains like in Italy, but there is one that is special and moves by animatronics. The Fountain of the Gods, in the Great Hall, has an Atlantis show with an epic battle filled with smoke, fire, lasers, and sound effects. The Gods even talk. The display depicts the fall of Atlantis, and sits atop of a 50,000-gallon aquarium. We used to go to my favorite restaurant there: Spago, by Wolfgang Puck, never with fewer than six people.

Prior to going to all the five-star restaurants we used to go to Ferraro's. It was a bit of a ride outside of the Strip but was worth the trip. It was a family run restaurant that treated you like family. On a visit we adored the battery-operated pepper mill that the waiter used, and we told the waiter we thought it was nice. The waiter was an Italian-American, maybe from Chicago, but not from Brooklyn, where I was from. He said, "You like it? I am selling them."

I looked at Faith and I chuckled.

Faith said, "I am sure your sister would want one."

The waiter said, "I'll be right back."

I said to Faith, "Oh boy, we are going to see his presentation."

The waiter returned with a new box and opened it in front of Faith and me. I said nothing, waiting to see his pitch. He pressed the button, and the pepper came out evenly.

He said, "Watch this," and he pressed another button. The pepper mill as it turned out was also a flashlight: it brightly illuminated our food.

"How do you like that?" I nodded. Then he went in for the close. " Do you know what the best part of this is? The instructions come in twenty languages."

I didn't want to laugh, since the waiter was so serious about selling.

"Only $90."

I wanted to tell the waiter he was crazy, but he was still serving us. I thanked him and that was the end of the conversation. I know he was upset, because he never said a word about the pepper mill after that. Faith said, "You know, if we would have bought one, the next thing coming out of the trunk of his car was going to be the furs." We both laughed.

Another property on the Strip was the Luxor Hotel, which had an Egyptian theme. The front of it had a hotel built on top of a pyramid with a light beam shooting to the sky. A New York-themed hotel eventually opened, and believe it or not, some New Yorkers went there to see the Statue of Liberty and the Manhattan skyline. Then Steve built the Wynn and the Encore, into which we eventually moved.

Bruce Eichner, a major New York City developer, hired us to help him in the design and leasing of the retail at the Cosmopolitan Hotel. That was a lot of fun. The casino was to be 90,000 square feet and we were doing the shops and restaurants around the casino.

In the three days of the conference, we were partying at night. My wife would join us on these trips and when she wasn't sitting poolside in the daytime, she came out with us at night. On a normal evening, we would go to the best restaurant in town and then go to see a show. Cirque Du Soleil had a show you didn't want to miss, with skilled acrobats, beautifully costumed players, and great music blended together around the property's theme. Some of the shows we saw were called *Love*, *Mystère*, and *Cirque du Soleil*. We also got to see some great concerts by Elton John, Cher, Barry Manilow, Céline Dion, and Rod Stewart.

These were the golden days of travel, and Las Vegas was a place where you wanted to go at least once a year.

I started having our Secret Broker Society dinners while everyone was attending ICSC, and we would pick a great restaurant. Who is the Secret Broker Society?

I saw a need to generate my own team of national and international brokers as a push-back to the larger firms that had small retail departments that were becoming larger. The number one rule was that you did not have to do deals with anyone, but you had to share information about your market. If you were not willing to do this, the group was not for you. I said this so members wouldn't feel the pressure of doing deals, but we did many deals together.

Monthly, we were doing calls. These brokers operated in 30 cities, and each month we had at least eight (8) to twelve (12) brokers on the phone. On the calls we would hear about everyone's market.

Dinner was held at Botero at the Wynn hotel, by the pool. We started at the bar with cocktails and then would have an amazing dinner—which really bonded the brokers. Everyone was in neutral territory and the brokers always thanked me for bringing them together. I didn't see any downside to promoting this group: only good. I managed to always get them good press. We had our spy logo, and people would ask us if we had a secret handshake.

At the start of our Las Vegas trips, Faith and I would then travel to

Beverly Hills, since we were already out West, and spend the Memorial Day weekend touring the shopping centers, visiting clients, then hitting the best restaurants. Faith would stay at the Peninsula Hotel on Wilshire Boulevard, and I would stay at the Four Seasons Hotel on Doheny Drive. We would always bump into stars like Julia Roberts, Suzanne Somers, Casey Kasem and, early on, even Jimmy Stewart. Wolf Blitzer from CNN used to have a cabana next to mine by the pool. Once I got married, my wife would join us.

We originally would take a flight from Vegas to Los Angeles, but one year I decided to drive through the desert and from that time on that's what we did: Faith in the back, the wife up front and the bags all in the trunk.

Our first stop before we went to our hotels was the Ivy Restaurant, the place to see or be seen on Melrose Drive. Champagne was always flowing, with great food and laughs. Faith liked my wife very much and my wife liked Faith the same. We all had tough backgrounds. My wife was a widow and shared the losses like Faith and I had. We all had a good understanding of our pasts and there was a tremendous amount of respect between the three of us. My wife always said she recognized my partnership with Faith, and she would never come between us, and she never did.

I always imagined that if Faith were to retire, I would take over the team and make sure she got a piece of every deal. But Suzanne always said Faith loved the business too much and would never retire. Many property owners still do deals in their 90s. I didn't know any brokers at that age still swinging the bat, but I imagined Faith would have been one of them.

XIII. TRUMP TOWER/TRUMP/IVANKA

Garrick Aug had become a popular commercial real estate broker-age company by this time. Charlie Aug was the first person to carve out a niche solely in retail leasing, and he led the industry in market share. Friends would always call me and tell me that wherever they went in Manhattan they would see "for rent" signs with my name on them. We knew all the retailers well. Faith's focus was international. Robert Futterman, the other rainmaker at the firm focused on national retailers. Robert represented all the Gap brands, and he did quite well for himself.

In New York there were six to eight important real estate families who owned a large chunk of the properties. We were representing most of them. One family that my firm represented was the Trump Organization.

Besides having retail at all their buildings, they owned Trump Tower on Fifth Avenue and 56th Street. We were representing Donald Trump before he was President of the United States.

Mr. Trump made a deal with the department store Bonwit Teller, which made way for him to develop Trump Tower. He built a magnificent skyscraper that has luxury apartments, offices, retail and restaurants. There are six or seven levels of retail inside the Trump Tower, besides the retailers outside. One of the retailers outside was a French tenant called Charles Jourdan, which sold luxury brand shoes. Inside the tower, was an additional 90,000 square feet of retail that included a restaurant.

We would meet with Mr. Trump on occasion. His company's offices took an entire floor within the commercial part of the tower. Trump's office was relatively modest in size. He had all the magazine covers that he had appeared on, along with all the newspapers he was featured in, framed and hanging on the walls. His office had a great view of Central Park. He hadn't taken over the skating rink yet, but one could clearly see the rink from his office, as it stood out in the middle of all the park's trees. It was no wonder he was so passionate about taking it over. In the past, the city ran it and hadn't done a good job.

Charles Jourdan was one of Trump's main Fifth Avenue tenants and they were in bankruptcy. Robert Futterman had Timberland for a replacement. I was still new at Garrick Aug and one day I found myself sitting between Robert and Faith—facing Mr. Trump.

Timberland had just started to become popular with the younger generation. Trump did not know who they were. He kept on asking why we were talking about Timberland when he had a tenant. Then finally I spoke up and said, "Mr. Trump you do not have a tenant. Charles Jourdan is in bankruptcy and soon they will be gone." He looked at me, smiled and shortly thereafter the conversation ended.

Timberland never made it as a tenant, but thirty days later Robert Futterman found Salvatore Ferragamo, the luxury shoe and apparel company, and they leased the Fifth Avenue store and they were there as a tenant at Trump Tower for quite a while.

Many years later, Donald Trump's daughter, Ivanka, hired Faith and me to do the roll-out of her jewelry stores. To this day I still haven't met her. We dealt solely with her CEO. We handled one of her stores on Madison Avenue and another store on Mercer Street in Soho.

By this time, Faith and I had left Garrick-Aug and moved to Douglas Elliman. On the last assignment, Ivanka's new CEO tried to cut our commission in half, even though we had an agreement with her company. Faith's mate of thirty plus years, Jerry, died during the negotiations and Faith never made it known to any of her customers including Ivanka. Faith was always professional and even if you were deathly ill, she told you not to say anything to anybody—thinking the client/customer might go elsewhere if they thought you were sick.

I wrote a lovely letter to Ivanka telling her that Faith's husband had died and that her CEO was looking to give us a big cut in our commission. One hour later, a basket of chocolates arrived addressed to Faith with a beautiful sympathy note from Ivanka, along with a check in the full amount of our commission.

She was a class act. I remember one time being at a fashion show and she was sitting on the other side of the runway—and I can say with all the fabulous models in the room, she was by far the prettiest woman under the tent. That was when the fashion shows were being held at Lincoln Center.

We had the funeral for Jerry. There had been no grave put aside for him, but Faith remembered that there was one spot still available, though smaller, in his family's plot. One of our vendors, Lorraine Kelly, who had worked at the city morgue in the past, found out which cemetery it was located in, and once we had held the memorial ceremony at Frank E. Campbell, we proceeded there.

Faith took Jerry's death badly. My wife and I made sure she always had company, taking her wherever we went. We always enjoyed our Sunday brunches together at Bar Italia, on Madison Avenue and East 66th Street. Years later, I arranged a photo shoot with Christian Johnson, the famous photographer. He shot a series inside and outside of the restaurant. There were a few pictures of us standing across the street and one would have thought it was in Vogue magazine.

Finally, Faith started dating and the gentlemen started to roll in on an assembly line: Luigi, Bill, Tony, and a few more. Faith was enjoying herself and I was happy she was moving forward with her life.

XIV: REUNITING WITH HARRY SCHWARTZ

Years later, I realized that practically every one of the managers who ran Harry Schwartz's gyms did not have a father living, and all of us had looked up to Harry as a role model. He had a fleet of fancy cars, like vintage Citroëns, Alfa Romeos, Ferraris, and Jaguars. He owned many of the properties the gyms were sitting on. He had built a company in a new field and he was in great shape. It wasn't hard to try to model yourself after him. But, by now Harry had retired and he had sold most of his shares in his company.

Here is how I got to reconnect with Harry. One day, I wrote a letter to Harry, thanking him for the reference letter he had given me when I left his company, and I went on to tell him about the success I was enjoying in real estate. I knew he lived in Atlantic Beach, N.Y., but I did not know the exact address. I decided, since his neighborhood was small and probably only had one or two postmen, I would simply write, "Harry Schwartz, Former President of Jack La Lanne," and the town and zip code. I figured that the postman knew Harry because he was so social.

One Sunday morning, I got a call from someone, whose voice I didn't recognize. He said, "Is this Joey Aquino?" And I said, yes, this is him. He said, "Do you know who this is?"

I said, "Well you are not my psychiatrist," always the one to be cheeky.

He said, "Oh, you have a psychiatrist?" Then he said, "This is Harry

Schwartz." I said, "Oh my God, Harry."

We talked for about 30 minutes. I told him all about my real estate successes and how I was working for a fabulous company, and I had a new mentor named Faith Hope Consolo and we were doing deals.

He replied, "Yes, I read all about it in your letter. I do not live in that house anymore in Atlantic Beach. I gave it to my ex-wife. Now, I am living with Jerry in Atlanta, Georgia."

Jerry ran the ladies service department of about 1,000 women at Jack La Lanne. She was a former beauty queen.

I said, "Harry, coincidently I am coming to Atlanta next month, let's get together," and we both agreed to meet.

The next month, Faith and I arrived in Atlanta to meet with property owners and take an overview of the market. I knew Harry loved bald eagles and I bought him a sculpture by Erté from The Shops in Trump Tower.

The meeting was in a restaurant at the Ritz Carlton Hotel. It was a lovely evening and we caught up nicely. Finally, Harry said, "I wish I had invited you both to the house." We agreed that I would come back again to have that visit.

Our meeting ended; we kept in touch, and sure enough several months later, I made the trip by myself back to Harry's home. This time I was a guest at his place for the weekend.

Harry's property was magnificent. It was on a 100-acre parcel with its own lake. It was on different levels: you drove off the main road and you eventually spiraled down to his lakeside house. The house was modest in size since there was only Jerry and Harry. Harry took me out on the lake the next afternoon in a small boat. I was about to put my hand in the water when he said, "Don't do that! A copperhead snake will bite your hand off." I pulled my arm back quickly.

That Sunday he had a regular visitor who would come every third week and it was a surprise to me: my former supervisor now lived in Atlanta and here he was, sitting in front of me at the breakfast table. It was he who had got me removed from John Wilton's area.

It was said, he had a bit of a drinking and drug problem. I thought he had one when we worked together, but now I heard the real story. He got promoted to a position in Pennsylvania and I believe he went into that market with the iron fist and forgot the velvet glove. Well, the staff there reported him to the head office, and they came down and gave him a drug test to see that he wasn't clean. They told him either to go to rehab or lose his job, and he agreed to go to rehab. When he was there, Harry volunteered to watch over him if they relocated him to Atlanta and sure enough, it was agreed. So, there he was, humbly sitting in front of me, not too happy to see me. He was married and they had two twin girls. I was happy for him, he had cleaned up.

I didn't overdo it, but I made sure he knew I was doing well after four years of being knocked around and that I landed nicely on my feet.

Lesson learned: Karma is real.

XV. BACK IN TIMES SQUARE/TOYS "R" US

Faith got a call from a major landlord, in Times Square, who wanted to meet her. He told her he had 108,000 square feet of space he wanted to lease. She invited me to come along to a meeting the following week—where the landlord told us his present broker Bradley Mendelsohn at CBRE wasn't producing and he was thinking of firing him. He asked us to come up with a plan and we agreed to meet the following week.

The following week, I had our ad agency, Miller Advertising, put together an ad campaign at a cost of $100,000. It incorporated 10 full-page ads to appear in various trade and local newspaper publications, including *Crain's*, the *New York Post*, *Real Estate Weekly*, and other big names, along with a brochure to be sent to all the tenants and brokers. The asking rent was $10 million a year and I said to myself, "What is $100,000, when you are hunting for $10 million, when it is used strictly for marketing?"

Christmas and New Year's came and went. It was January and the owner said he was not ready to decide. But by February, we got called back and he was ready to go.

We immediately put together the ad campaign, hung the sign on the property, and mailed out high-gloss marketing brochures with inserts and all the bells and whistles. All the costs were incurred by the property owner.

Things were moving quickly and about eight weeks into the assignment, Faith made a statement in the *New York Post*, simultaneously with the ads appearing, that the space was available, and that the street reminded her of the *Champs Elysées*. Everyone knows that street in Paris. How can you not? It's Paris's Fifth Avenue? She got an angry phone call from the property owner, saying she was not authorized to make that statement and he wanted to fire us. I was home in Brooklyn and got this frantic call from Faith telling me what transpired.

I told her to get the property owner on the phone. We had a three-way conversation and I believe our company attorney was on the call too.

*THE NEW YORK POST ARTICLE *

MOSS TIES UP 'BOWTIE BLDG.' PLANS By Steve Cuozzo Published May 9, 2000, 4:00 a.m. ET J Sign Up THE Moss family finally means to do something with its weird but wonderful Times Square building at 1530 Broadway. Owner Charles B. Moss Jr. has called in Garrick-Aug's crack retail leasing team of Vice-Chairman Faith Hope Consolo and Managing Director Joseph Aquino. You know the Moss site: the ramshackle-looking, low-slung jumble of tourist and fast-food shops topped by a cacophony of colorful billboards. It's an anachronism in the New Times Square, flanked by giants like the glittering Bertelsmann and Conde Nast buildings. Two years ago, Moss backed out of a near-deal with Bertelsmann to develop a second tower on its site. He found he could make more money just leasing sign space, to the tune of a reported $50 million. Last December, Charles' son, Ben Moss, told us the property would be emptied by February for conversion to one first-class retail space. That didn't happen. But now, *Consolo says, "We're going to make the Moss property into a blockfront*

on the Champs Elysees.*"* Existing tenants of the "Bowtie Building," including the UA movie theater, have left or are leaving. There will be $1 million in interior demolition and construction "to create a new plate" at the "world's most exciting retail/TV studio opportunity in the heart of Times Square."

* END OF ARTICLE*

In our agreement, we needed an approval on anything said to the press, but something smells fishy. The statement had been positive and the owner still wanted to let us go. In our phone conversation, I realized that there was no way we were going to change his mind, so I said, "If you want to fire us, you have to buy us out, since we did 90 percent of the work and now it's our time to pick the low-hanging fruit."

He said, "What do you want?"

I said, "One million dollars."

He balked and then said; "I'll get back to you." That call happened on a Friday afternoon and on Monday Lee Stand, our General Counsel, walked into Faith's office and said, he offered us $275,000, I think we should take it. We accepted. That Friday we received the check. Faith and I knew that there was something more to this. No one hands you a check for this amount of money to fire you.

Three weeks later, Faith and I were at ICSC, in Las Vegas, and a man approached Faith. He worked for a property owner on 42nd Street in Times Square. He congratulated Faith for snatching Toys "R" Us for the Bowtie Building. He said that he was working with them on his property and then one day they just stopped negotiating and he saw they had come over to her property. Faith told me what had transpired. I responded to Faith, "I guess Toys "R" Us saw our $100,000 cost of

113

marketing."

She replied, "How could they not? The ads were in every major trade and local newspaper and we had a 100 foot sign on the building." Prior, there was no visible marketing that I knew of.

We went back to the office and told our house counsel what we had found out and we all agreed to stay quiet till the deal was done.

By the end of the summer, the deal was announced and Toys "R" Us signed a lease for 108,000 square feet. Immediately, Garrick Aug sued for $6 million. The property owner's right-hand person called up our attorney and said, "What's up with the lawsuit? We gave you $275,000 and you signed a release." Our attorney said, "Yes, but you didn't tell us you had a deal out with Toys "R" Us and if you had told us, we wouldn't have taken the money." The call ended.

During the discovery period of a lawsuit, documents are passed among the parties so that everyone can review the evidence of the other party. Sure enough, the property owner's attorney sent us the initial Toys "R" Us offer. We read it and it was clear it was submitted during the time of our exclusive agency period. It was sent to the property owner by the former brokers of the property. The letter was signed by David LaPierre and Bradley Mendelsohn was cc'd. The offer should have been sent to us, since we were the new exclusive brokers. But instead, they sent it directly to the property owner.

Years later, when I returned to CBRE looking for a global position, I finally got an interview with a second person who told me his full-time job was arbitrating broker disputes. That immediately turned me off. At Garrick-Aug, we had just three arbitrations over a fourteen-year period — and now I was being told it's a regular occurrence.

It took several years to get to court. When we did have our day in court, the judge made it clear she was not going to waste any time on this case after she saw the evidence and strongly recommended that we settle right there and then. The property owner of the Bowtie Building gave their initial offer of $500,000. I told her I wasn't authorized to accept it and had to call my office. I called Lee Stand and he was excited. He said, "Should we take it?"

I said, "Let me go back and see if we can get a million."

He said, "Okay, go get them!"

The judge asked to see the property owners and his team in her chambers. After the meeting, we returned in front of the judge's bench and the property owner said they were ready to make an offer of $700,000.

"Your Honor, let me make another call to the office."

I went back to Lee and he said, "Good going."

I said, "I think we should take it." Lee agreed and I went back and told the judge.

The week prior to the court case, that broker had moved to another large brokerage firm. I thought that was strange, but maybe not, since he had been with his previous firm for more than two decades. I always wondered if the property owner had a clause in his commission agreement that the broker would have to return the commission if Garrick Aug sued and won. That will always be a mystery to me.

It was not every day in my business that I made one million dollars, but it was the early 1990s, when the market was hot, and that is what I did. I negotiated both parts of the settlements and I was pleased. This was a far cry from when I was selling perfumes for three dollars apiece on Park Avenue South between classes.

Those brokers went on to win the Deal of the Year award from the Real Estate Board of New York (REBNY). Faith and I some years later visited the REBNY offices and mentioned it to Eileen Spinola, who was senior vice president at REBNY, and she just shrugged her shoulders. It wasn't ethical, how they went about it, but that's how our business goes and it appeared REBNY just didn't care.

115

Toys "R" Us built a beautiful 108,000-square foot store with a Ferris wheel inside. This was the beginning of the repositioning of Times Square.

XVI. THE ONE THAT GOT AWAY

Abe Hirschfeld owned 320 East 61st Street, where the Vertical Club was a tenant. That was where I worked for six months prior to leaving Jack La Lanne's and Bally Fitness and entering real estate. Abe was an unconventional man. He ran for the United States Senate and lost once he had made his millions from investing in parking garages.

I was still friends with many Jack LaLanne Health Club employees and my friend Jason Pacelli still worked for them. He mentioned that the Vertical Club lease was coming available. At that time, I was working with a health club chain called Town Sports International, doing business as Reebok.

We made an offer to Abe's son. Shortly thereafter, we arranged for him to meet the tenant and we were negotiating. The Vertical Club still had some time on the lease and Abe's son told us he was not able to make the deal.

Months went by, and we learned that the Hirschfeld organization had done a deal with Town Sport. When we sued, we saw the new lease was on the same business terms as what we had offered. During the lawsuit period, Abe Hirschfeld was convicted for arranging to have his business partner Stanley Stahl murdered. Abe was imprisoned and on the day of the trial, he appeared in court wearing his orange prison outfit. It was surreal.

The outcome was not good for us. Even though our offer matched exactly where the deal got struck, it appeared that Abe was no longer speaking to his son during that period. We sued for $3.5 million and got nothing. The judge felt there was no connection to Abe and my firm since he was not talking to his son and we weren't talking to Abe. That's how crazy the business was. When selling residential homes & apartments, you go to the closing and you get a check and the seller says "thank you." That doesn't happen all the time in commercial real estate.

XVII. MADISON AVENUE

Faith got a call from Marjorie Nesbit to represent her in the leasing of 717 Madison Avenue. The stores had low ceilings. On one side was Devi Kroell, who was known for her snakeskin handbags and shoes; the other store was available to be rented. The storefronts were landmarked, and they were made from copper. This was an unusual element for a storefront to be made of, but Marjorie was determined to restore them and we were excited by her plans. We recommended she take out a portion of the second floor to give her higher ceilings, and she did.

It was the height of summer, and I came up with a marketing effort to give a car away to the broker who made the deal. Marjorie liked the idea. We chose a Mini Cooper and I came up with an ad campaign slogan that sent out the message to the brokers: "Give Us Your Max, We Give You a Mini."

We ran ads in all the trades and had a broker party. The local Mini Cooper dealership had driven a car to the property and we had it parked outside the store with a big ribbon on it. Again, our marketing was unique: To this day, no one gives gifts out like that.

The marketing lasted for six months and finally, Faith and I leased the store to Soigné K. Soigné Kothari was from India. She came from an affluent diamond dealer family. Originally Soigné was going to partner with an Indian designer, Kimaya, but decided to do it on her own.

Soigné was catering to the affluent Indian community for their weddings. Indian weddings can go on for days and a woman needs several outfits for the event. Up to this point, if an Indian lady wanted to get dressed for a wedding, she had to go to Boston or Chicago for her dresses.

Even though we gave a Mini Cooper as an incentive, none of the brokers made offers that we considered substantial. Tincati, a luxury menswear brand from Milan, made an offer through an Italian broker, Guglielmo Pernis, but it was too low. After the deal, Marjorie was kind enough to award the car to us.

XVIII. JULIA SPERATORE

Friends of mine who were huge opera lovers started inviting me to join them at the Metropolitan Opera. I would meet them every other week. One day, Dr. Zimmerman told me that for the next season he had a single first-row seat that I could buy from him: seventeen shows in total. I jumped at the chance.

He said, "But there's a catch. You're going to be sitting next to Julia Speratore, she's an opera teacher. She's 92 years old and I drove her home after the show. Would you mind doing the same? She lives nearby, in the Ansonia hotel residences."

I knew exactly where that was located: about 10 blocks north from Lincoln Center. The famous opera singer, Enrico Caruso was known to have lived there as Babe Ruth the famous Yankee slugger ball player of the past.

The night arrived, for the first night of the 17 shows, and I met Julia. She was as chatty as could be and flirted with the men who walked by. She was also friendly with the women, once telling a young lady next to us that she had lovely legs.

One day, she called and asked my assistant if she could speak to me. Nancy said, "There's a Julia Speratore on the phone. She says she knows you from the opera."

I answered, "Julia, how are you?"

"Yes, this is Julia Speratore and I must apologize, I found your card in my pocketbook. Who are you?"

I chuckled, knowing Julia's age, and I reminded her where she had seen me.

"Oh yes, that's right, how are you?" Then she went in for the close: "When are you coming for voice lessons?"

I laughed and replied, "Julia, I don't sing." Julia was persistent and I had to make believe I had another call to get her off the phone.

Weeks went by. I had met Julia at the opera several more times, and then had driven her home. Then I got another phone call from her. She asked again, "I found your business card in my apartment, who are you?" Once I reminded her who I was, she replied, "Right, so when are you coming for lessons?"

I replied, "Julia, I told you I don't sing."

"Nonsense, everyone can sing."

Her persistence got my curiosity up, and I asked her how much she charged. She said, "Fifteen dollars." I couldn't believe that number.

Always looking for a bargain, I said, "Ok, I'll try one."

That following Tuesday evening, there I was at the *Belle époque*-designed Ansonia apartment building. The Ansonia was originally built as a hotel. Julia's apartment had high ceilings and her windows were two French door panels, like those you see in France or Italy. She had a baby grand piano next to these windows and she was sitting behind it playing a tune that I recognized from *La Traviata*.

She said, "Okay, let's go up and down the scales. Follow me: Ma, Mae, Mee, Moe, Moo." For the next 10 minutes, she went up and down the scales and I sang along. Then, she took out a book of sheet music from Vaccai and together we sang my first opera song while she played the piano. We did this for another 10 minutes. She was teaching me how to breathe and on the high notes, how to pull my stomach in to help me hit the high notes. In fact, she would point to my stomach when I had to pull it in.

Finally, she stopped, and the room went silent. You could have heard a pin drop. Julia was wearing a Gap t-shirt and a hat and a pair of eyeglasses that she looked over as they hung off the tip of her nose. The glasses were halved lenses just for reading and wondering where this was going. She asked, "Do you like what you are doing?"

"I love the way I am singing Julia, I am having so much fun."

Then, she went in for the close; remember her age.

"Can you come every Tuesday at 7:30?"

I looked at her and smiled, and said;

"Julia I would love to come every Tuesday at 7:30."

There you go. For the next two years, I was a student of Julia's.

Julia had about 15 students and they all loved her. At Christmas, we had a potluck party with only one condition: You had to sing for your supper, and everyone did.

Julia passed away at 95, and all her students went to her memorial service at a church in Brooklyn. Everyone got up and gave their Julia story. I still had a recording of her voice that I brought and played, in which she wished me a Happy Easter. Some of the students cried when they heard it.

Julia never married, and she had a photo of her teacher on the wall above her piano. She always referred to him as "the Maestro." I am not sure if they ever had more of a relationship than a teacher and student, but it was clear that she loved this man dearly.

I managed to get her ticket when she passed, so I had a pair of first-row seats at the Metropolitan Opera. I wrote to The Met saying my Aunt

Julia moved to my residence. Yes, a white lie, but I paid for the tickets for at least the next fifteen seasons being right in the front row. If you were friends with me back then, it was sure that you were going to see at least one opera with me or you were getting a pair for yourself to enjoy. I loved going and I really got immersed in the music and the stories. I have my favorites like everyone else. I loved *La Traviata*, *La Boheme*, *Rigoletto*, *Tosca* and *Carmen*. When you are an opera lover, you can see the same ones over and over.

Lesson learned, no matter how old you are, like Julia, don't forget your ABCs: Always Be Closing!

XIX. CARLOS SLIM

In 2012, we were marketing the building where Elizabeth Taylor and Michael Todd, her third husband, lived back in the 1950s: 10 West 56th Street, a beautiful five-story brownstone with an elevator that was converted to commercial from residential. The Japanese company Felissimo called it their store for years.

We were marketing it for some time, getting bridal and hair salons, but none of those tenants had the credit to make the Japanese owners pull the trigger to go to lease.

One day, a broker Roxana Girand took a Spanish group to see it. Shortly thereafter, we found out it was one of Carlos Slim's companies. During this period, he was one of the richest men in the world. One of his major assets was Mexico's telephone company.

Carlos hit hard and quickly, and you had to be ready to move at their pace if you wanted to do a deal with them, or you would lose it. The deal went from contract to closing within five days to the tune of $15.5 million, but that wasn't without getting them up from their original $9 million offer. I took the final conference call with three other men. One was Alejandro; another was Carlos, who didn't speak; the third person was Arturo. I would like to assume that the person who was named Carlos on the phone was Mr. Slim, but I can only guess.

I did some bluffing. I had to give the push back, especially since we were asking $20 million, but nowhere in hell were we ever going to do that deal for $9 million. When they wanted a response as to why the $9 million wasn't accepted, I told them, "He threw the offer in the basket and walked out of the room."

Originally, I think they were going to make this property their Northeast headquarters, but that never transpired. They closed in five days and kept it vacant for about a year, finally leasing it to a hair salon.

Lesson learned: be ready for "fast and furious." Try not to blink.

XX. THE WORLD TRADE CENTER

Larry Silverstein controlled the Twin Towers at The World Trade Center when they came under attack by terrorists. The Port Authority owned the properties, but Larry had a long-term lease. After the properties were destroyed, Larry had to rebuild.

One day Larry called on Faith and me and invited us to his office. The new WTC buildings had retail at the base; they were almost finished. Larry wanted us to look over the plans.

We entered his conference room and his staff served us milk and warm chocolate chip cookies, I chuckled. Larry was sitting in front of us. I said, "Larry, no one ever served us chocolate chip cookies and milk, ask us whatever you want." He smiled and he did. He took out the plans for the retail stores for the new towers to be built and asked for us to review and to have our comments.

After we gave him our analysis, I said,

"Larry, now I have a question for you. How did you get started?"

Now, from what I recall — and remember, I'm approaching 70 — Larry replied:

Larry smiled and went on to tell us how his dad had worked for Helmsley Spear as an office leasing broker and when Larry came into the business, he worked with him. On Larry's first office deal, at the closing table, his customer announced that if he wanted to conclude the trans-

127

action, Larry had to share his commission with the customer's broker friend. Larry became furious, but he agreed and closed the deal. Upon returning to his office, he announced to his dad that he hated brokerage and that they were going to become landlords.

Whether this was folklore or how he started, he proceeded with his story. For the next 18 months, any time Larry spoke to a property owner, he would ask if their building was for sale. He learned of many properties, but he didn't have the cash deposit to secure any of them. Finally, he found one that was mostly vacant that was inexpensive because of its vacancy level. He needed just 15 percent which in today's market is a small deposit. He scoured the market talking to friends, family and colleagues and raised the money. Now, he had to find the rest of the money to close and make the property his. Larry told us he went to every bank in Manhattan and everyone turned him down. One day he had a meeting on Orchard Street. I mentioned that street earlier in the book, it's a street relatively known for inexpensive discounted merchandise. At the turn of the last century, it was known of peddlers selling their goods on wooden carts that wheeled down the street. The merchandise barrel changed a century later, only now they were sold in stores. He noticed a bank he had never heard of in the corner of his eye. Orchard Street is off the beaten path for any commercial real estate broker. But Larry happened to be in the neighborhood, and there was this bank he had never known existed. He entered the bank and showed the officer his business plan—which was badly worn from his pitches to the other banks. The gentleman said, "Okay, I like it, let me show this to my people and I'll call you in a few days."

A few days went by and the gentlemen called and told Larry that the bank was willing to lend him the money—and gave him the terms. Larry went back to his father with the good news and they both agreed that the terms were favorable. They agreed to go ahead with the loan. Simultaneously, around this period, when Larry was giving documents to the bank to get the loan approved, one of the top brokers from Helmsley Spear called Larry and told him that they knew he was in contract. They told Larry the address of the property and the exact terms of Larry's deal including the price and down payment. They went on to offer $100,000 over the contract to Larry to purchase it. Larry admitted that he was young and the $100,000 was like several millions of dollars in today's market. Larry immediately ran into his father's office and told him the news. The father sat and listened to Larry's excitement at how they would flip the contract and not worry about leasing this vacant office building.

Larry's father waited patiently till Larry finished with his story. Then he said, "Son, please go tell those nice people we are not selling the building. You did well getting us this deal. We are going to become landlords now."

That, Larry said, was how they became property owners. In the next few buildings, they raised money from friends and family. Once they got some experience in operating, they went to insurance companies for financing and the rest is history.

Imagine: Larry put this all together because he got screwed on his first leasing deal!

Lesson learned: You can accomplish anything if you put your mind to it, even if you get screwed.

Larry, shortly after this meeting, invited us to go on his boat. I am not a seafaring person, but I felt obliged to go, and I wasn't sorry. The boat must have been over 200 feet long, I wasn't counting, but it was huge. Larry invited a large group of New York City brokers for a cruise around Manhattan. His crew provided everyone with skip sneakers so they didn't scratch the deck. Larry is truly a gentleman. My fathers name was Anthony, but for some reason, everyone called him Larry. I shared this story with Larry, a few times over the years and every time I did, Larry would smile.

Years later, when I started my own firm, he was kind enough to sponsor my company to the Real Estate Board of New York (REBNY), the most prestigious real estate organization in the State of New York and maybe the world.

XXI. MY FRIEND BRIAN/BUENOS AIRES

My family moved several times when we lived in Brooklyn. The fourth property Mom and Dad owned was a 50- by 100-foot lot with a non detached house on a nice tree-lined block in East Flatbush, Brooklyn. A waitress who served my wife and I referred to it now as "The Hood." My wife and I recently saw Diana Ross do a concert at The Kings Theatre near my old home, and we felt totally safe there.

Most of the people on the block in the 60's and 70's were Irish and some were German. I like to joke that when our Italian family arrived, the neighbors must have said, "There goes the neighborhood!"

We had just left Midwood, which was predominantly a Jewish neighborhood. The Yeshiva of Flatbush was near my home and most of the property owners of Manhattan went to that school. Midwood was known for the famous people who grew up there, such as Woody Allen. When Woody wrote and produced movies, it was about all the neighborhood people there. I knew most of the character types that he portrayed in his movies, since they were my neighbors. My family was forced to move, since the city was going to build a high school on our block. The school they planned to build was named after the radio announcer Edward R. Morrow.

East Flatbush, where we now lived, was famous for the movie *The Lords of Flatbush*. We had our share of movie and recording stars there too, like Barbra Streisand, Neil Diamond and even the businessman

Howard Shultz, the CEO of STARBUCKS even lived nearby . I am a baby-boomer and on my new block, every other house had kids my age, so there was never a problem to get a half a dozen guys or more together to play stickball, football, or hockey. Brian Boland was a dear friend of mine who eventually became the altar boy at my sister's wedding. We were close.

Years later, on the weekend leading up to the Fourth of July, I decided to look him up. There was no internet back then: only the phone book. I investigated the Manhattan directory and sure enough, there he was, working downtown as a lawyer in a prestigious law firm. Brian had gone to Cornell.

I called the receptionist and asked for him. She replied, "Oh, I am so sorry, Brian doesn't work here anymore."

Before she could hang up, I said, "Please, I am Brian's childhood friend. He lived directly across the street from me and he was even the altar boy to my sister's wedding. Please give me his phone number."

How could she refuse? She said, "No worries," and when she returned to the line, she said, "He moved to Kansas City and here's the phone number." I said to myself, *Phew, if I didn't call, I never would have found him in Kansas.* Knowing the phone books back then were changed every year.

I called on the Friday leading up to a holiday weekend, and he wasn't there. I left a voicemail. By the following Tuesday, by which time I had forgotten that I had left the message, my secretary told me that there was a Brian on the phone.

I picked up the phone and we reunited. He said, "Joe Aquino, how the hell did you find me? I am in Kansas." I told him how I started with the Yellow Pages. Brian told me he would be in Manhattan in six months and that he wanted to get together. He would have his wife with him and he would love for me to meet her.

I said, "Great!" Six months later, I met Brian and his wife and to no surprise, she reminded me of his sisters and mom.

A year went by. I got a call from Brian telling me that I was getting divorced. I felt terrible. He said, "I am moving back to New York."

I said, "That's great, do you have a job?" He said, "Yes.

I'll be at 101 Park Avenue."

I paused, then replied, "Brian. I'm working at 99 Park." The boy that lived across from me, now was working across the street from me.

Every third Friday, we would meet and have a guy's night out. We enjoyed going to Bar Six on Sixth Avenue and 13th Street. They always had a lively bunch there.

Brian called me one day and said, "Do you want to come with me to visit my sister Denise? She is a U.S. Diplomat who lives in Chile." I said, "Yes, of course. That would be great to see your sister and visit Chile"

We went to visit Denise and her husband Alejandro, who was an Argentine. We met them at their home outside of Santiago, Chile and stayed a few days, then drove through the Andes mountains to Mendoza and took a plane to Buenos Aires. This trip inspired me to become a world traveler.

Alejandro raised an Argentine horse breed called Falabella. They are miniature horses, but unlike many other miniature horse breeds, the Fallabella's head is in proportion to its body, rather than disproportionately large.

Alejandro had 400 heads of Falabellas at his ranch. His crew consisted of four gauchos on normal-size horses, corralling them. Alejandro had the gauchos gallop the entire herd our way and they stopped once they got to the fence behind which we were standing.

After this spectacular event, I looked to my right and saw a 40-foot conference table. I asked Alejandro, "Who are the smartest people you've ever dealt with, in terms of nationality?"

"The Dutch." I said, "Of course, they were the original bankers."

"Who's the toughest?"

Alejandro's face turned sour. "Those friggin Japanese. For two years, they sent two different people here to look over the horses every month for the weekend. Never once did they smile. Finally, after two years of them coming every month, I told them to take the fucking horses and get off my ranch."

Lesson learned: There are various ways to close, and one is by wearing out your opponent.

When I entered Santiago and went through customs, the agent asked me for *"cinco pesos."* I had gone to Aviation High School, which was overseen by the Federal Aviation Administration. We weren't required to take a language course, since we had to take four to five additional periods of shop daily in addition to the five Regents' subjects, and I didn't want to stay for an additional period to learn a language. I was also on the school's track team and there were only so many hours in a day. So, I passed on taking the foreign language class. The agent looked at my name, *Aquino.* It's a Spanish name, but it's also Italian. He said something which I knew wasn't nice. I didn't have to understand exactly what he said, but I knew it was something like, "I can't believe this guy with a name like *Aquino* doesn't speak one word of Spanish." Well, after this incident, I said to myself, "He's right. I should know a second language." On my return to New York, I enrolled in an Italian class and have been studying the language ever since.

I was dying to meet someone and get married. In fact, a year prior, I went to a soothsayer, and she said I was going to meet my bride at a religious function. Believing her, I started going back to Sunday church services.

Brian and I went to a buffet dinner at the Toy Building at 200 Fifth Avenue. The party was in celebration of St. Patrick's Day, which is hugely celebrated in New York City. We got in line and filled our plates with good portions of turkey with all the trimmings. Brian walked over to a table that had seats for 10. Two of the chairs were unavailable, they had handbags hanging on the backs. Brian turned to me and said, "Sit."

"Brian, these chairs are taken."

"Nonsense. If those girls wanted these seats, they would be here. Sit."

Well, Brian was firm, so I allowed him to sit me down next to this beautiful girl with upswept blonde hair and grey eyes. Her name was Suzanne. I said hello and for the next three hours, neither one of us could shut up.

She was from Northern Ireland. Her accent wasn't the traditional one you hear from the south. Northern Ireland is one of the constituent countries that form part of the United Kingdom, and there was a distinct difference in her accent.

She had come to America on a Morrison Visa she won back home. She was widowed and I told her that I had lost my parents at a young age. We exchanged condolences. The friends she was with were from Ireland; they were sitting across the table from us: a beautiful array of blonde and redheads with lovely smiles. These were special people. I asked Suzanne to dance, and she said no. Later I found out she was wearing uncomfortable shoes. Finally, it came time to close the deal.

I asked her for her number and she paused. It was the longest pause of my life. I knew the first person to talk first lost, *you remember my earlier lesson*, so I kept silently saying quietly to myself, "Give me your number, give me your number..." I used to do this when I was selling memberships. Then I would say, *"Fill out the card, fill out the card."*

Finally, she said, "I don't have a pen."

"I have one."

"I don't have paper."

"I do!" and took out my business card and handed it to her.

On the back of it she gave her work number. I still have that card today. The girls whose chairs we were sitting in, eventually came over to recover their pocketbooks, but I had secured Suzanne's phone number by then. Now, it was time for everyone to go home.

Our first date was terrific. I took her to see a Sarah Brightman concert at Radio City after going to dinner at the Cub Room in Soho. After the concert, I wanted to drive her home (she lived in White Plains), but she insisted she take the train from Grand Central Station. Not knowing whether my new friend knew how dangerous Grand Central could be on a Saturday night, I said, "Okay, but allow me to put you on the train." She agreed. Well, there we were on the tracks, and I felt like I was in that Al Pacino movie, *Carlito's Way*—only now, I was the dark-haired lead – with my beautiful blonde date.

I remember like it was yesterday. She was wearing a pearl grey silk top with a narrow belt of the same material tied around her waist. The train was pulling into the station. This was its last stop before turnaround. I put my arms around her waist and I got my first kiss. It was great. We stopped and looked into each other's eyes. It felt wonderful!

The next week, she went back home to Ireland to visit her family and the following week, I went to Club Med in Mexico with my good friend Jason. During that week I found that I was sick and tired of the singles scene. Young and middle-aged women were dancing on the tables, swinging beer bottles and glasses of tequila. I knew at this point my unmarried days were numbered.

When I returned home, I called Suzanne and we scheduled our second date. We went to a restaurant called Cibo near my Manhattan apartment. I had a house in Brooklyn with a pool, but stayed at this *pied-à-terre* during the week. After a lovely dinner I invited her up to see photos of a trip that I had just taken with my sister to Italy. That was the only thing we did and then I took her back to Grand Central Station again for her to catch her train home.

We dated for the next five months and I knew she must be wondering why I wasn't making a move. I really wanted to build the trust factor and I knew exactly what I was doing. One day in the car, she made a reference to this subject and I said, "Don't worry, I am willing to wait a year."

She immediately said, "A year? Oh, that's not necessary."

Bam, the deal was sealed. Shortly thereafter, I asked her to marry me. She told me her girlfriend had asked her what she would do if I proposed. She had said, "I think I will say yes." And she did.

When we went to see her folks for the first time, we decided to keep our engagement a surprise. I had my dear friend Andrew Miller, of Miller Advertising, make me a T-shirt with the following message on the front:
   "Eileen and Pat, may I have Suzanne's hand in marriage?"
I told Andrew only to include the "Yes" checkbox. He laughed and said, "Sure." Knowing how the Irish love a good joke, I figured they'd appreciate my sense of humor.

The only problem was that I had to carry the engagement ring in my pocket during the flight from London to Belfast, and I was nervous it might fall out. It was my first time in London and Suzanne really showed me the town. We stayed near Harrods across the street from Hyde Park where Princess Diana had lived. The hotel was called The Milestone.

When I met my father-in-law at the airport, we hit it off right away.

137

There wasn't a cloud in the sky, and the sun was beaming down. He pulled me aside and said, "Joe, it's not like this every day." We both laughed.

They took us to lunch at a lovely hotel. I was sitting on one of the coziest couches having lunch, constantly checking my pocket to see if the ring was still there. We finally arrived at their home. I was so nervous, I nodded to my wife, letting her know I was going into the living room to have my talk with her dad. She smiled and said, "Go ahead."

I turned to Pat and asked, "Do you wear glasses?"

He replied, "Yes, why?"

I said, "Go get them."

When he returned, I took off my button-down shirt to reveal the T-shirt and said, "Pat, read my shirt."

He did—and with a shout, called out to his wife, "Eileen, get me a pen!" She answered, "Sure, Pat, I'll be right in!" I think she knew what was happening.

With pen in hand, he paused, looked me in the eye, and said, "But Joe, I don't have a dowry to give you."

Totally touched, that he should say this.

I immediately replied, "Pat, I don't want your dowry—I want your daughter." He smiled, said "Okay Joe," he got down on one knee and checked off the box.

The year after we got married, Brian moved to the Carolinas. He was part of my wedding party. I felt he came back into my life just for me to meet my bride. It seemed to me that Brian married everyone off in my family, my sisters being the first when he was the altar boy.

I realized that the soothsayer was right after all: I did meet my wife at a religious function, since it was a St. Patrick's Day party.

We were married September 5, 2002, in Westbury on Long Island. We found a catering hall called Carlton on the Park that was situated on a golf course. Suzanne's family came in from Northern Ireland and it was a beautiful day. The Carlton had been recently renovated and being on a golf course was the closest thing to Ireland, since everywhere you looked was green. Our friend Liz had gotten married there the year before and we had fallen in love with the place. We had about 120 people, of which 20 were children.

The first thing I did when I knew we were getting married was to book the honeymoon. My wife asked, "Why did you do that?"

I replied, "I am not sure how much the wedding is going to cost, but I want to have a first-class honeymoon." We did. We went to Rome and stayed at the Eden Hotel. From its restaurant on the top floor, you can see the cupola of St. Peter's Basilica, one mile away: a clear view, so romantic.

We only stayed in Rome three days before we moved on. I had many places to show my wife before we left. We visited the Roman Forum, the Colosseum, the Spanish Steps, Castel Sant' Angelo, the Piazza Navona, the Pantheon, the Trevi Fountain and then St. Peter's in the Vatican, which included the Sistine Chapel.

We then drove to Positano in a rented Alfa Romeo. When you get to the Amalfi Coast it feels like there are 100 bends and turns on the road.

At first, you drive like you are Mario Andretti, the race car driver, but after the 35th turn, you drive like you just finished running a marathon in the heat.

Finally, my wife was convinced we had passed the hotel, because we were driving endlessly. I assured her we still had a way to go. Then, out of the corner of my eye I saw a very small sign on the left-hand side which said San Pietro Hotel. I had almost missed it. I entered the parking lot. I said, "We are here."

An extraordinarily handsome man approached the car and opened the door to my wife's side and said, "Benvenuto." He was obviously Italian, wearing Ray Ban sunglasses, a nice tan, chinos, and a tan hip-length zip jacket. My wife wouldn't get out. The parking lot was on a cliff.

I said,, "Get out, we are here."

"No, I am not getting out. We are not here, where's the hotel?"

Then I said, more firmly, "Get out — we're here."

She was right: there was no visible sign of the hotel. We were having our first marital spat.

She said, " No, I am not getting out."

I said in a louder tone, "Don't embarrass me, get out," confirming I had read the sign correctly. She cautiously got out.

Mr. Benvenuto — or whatever his name was — walked us to the *ascensore* and pressed a button. The elevator descended, and within seconds its doors opened onto a beautiful lobby with a panoramic view of the Mediterranean Sea. Well, the smile returned to my wife's face, and it didn't leave for the rest of the week.

The hotel had been built into the side of a mountain, with the parking lot at the very top. Positano's pace was much slower than Rome's, with its charming seaside atmosphere and beachside calm. We truly enjoyed our time there.

One day we drove to Ravello and had lunch on a hill overlooking a lemon grove. My wife still talks about that meal, on a terrace adjacent to the town's church. She always says, *"When I looked out into the lemon grove, I felt like I was looking at heaven."*

On Sunday, we attended Mass and listened to the service in Italian. On our last evening, we had dinner at Le Sirenuse, where the entire restaurant was lit by candlelight. Before we left, we bought two beautifully hand-designed ceramic pots, which are still displayed in our home today. They shipped them to us in a crate.

We took a hydroplane from Naples to Capri and stayed at the Quisisana Hotel for a night. My father's family was from Naples, and they had come to the United States in the early 1900s. I could feel my family's presence there and tried to imagine how it must have felt to leave their homeland, never to return. Capri was lovely, with plenty of shops and a wide choice of fine restaurants. I bought a pair of racing car shoes from Tod's that I still own today.

Years later, I met the owner of Tod's, Diego Della Valle, at the Financial Times Luxury Summit in Rome. I told him I still had those beautiful shoes from Capri. Seventeen years had passed, and he, being a true shoe salesman, smiled and said, *"Joe, that's fine that you love my shoes — but you have to go to the store and buy more."*

I have, of course — but that pair from our honeymoon still has a shine I can't quite explain. Every time I wear them, they make me smile.

141

XXII. THE DOUGLAS ELLIMAN YEARS

All good things come to an end. Charlie Aug decided it was time to sell his company. At that point, Robert Futterman had left and taken his team with him and opened his own company that was doing extremely well.

Charlie needed a heart transplant and he didn't survive the operation. He must have known he was sick and that it was time for him to sell. He offered Faith and me the company for $3 million, but she had no interest in buying, nor did I. Charlie spoke to everyone in the industry and soon we started to do the same, but Faith was looking for us to exit.

Charlie found a buyer in the investment banking field. Faith just did not like him. Faith and I had attended Howard Rubenstein's 50th anniversary party at Tavern on the Green. Howard's company was one of the best public relation firms around, representing a lot of real estate companies, plus the New York Yankees and the Archdiocese of New York.

Esther Mueller, a dear friend of Faith's, introduced Faith to Dotty Herman, who was one of the partners of Prudential Douglas Elliman. The two hit it off and the romance started.

In weeks to come, Faith also met with Dotty's partner, Howard Lorber, but I was not part of any of the negotiations. Finally, Faith said, "I made my deal with Douglas Elliman and now you have to go up and make yours." I wasn't pleased to hear this. I felt we should have made our deal together.

I went to negotiate with Howard Lorber but I didn't have much leverage. He said, "I see you as the COO of Faith's team," but that's as far as I got.

In effect, Lorber was right. Faith only went to the initial pitch or follow-up meetings; she never showed space or did tours to show the retailers the marketplace. I did all that. I was the guy who went into the field, while she stood back and watched the store and pushed the deals along the way. They bought Faith, but I had to deliver on the promise.

The marketing department at Douglas Elliman did artwork that they were going to send out. It was a cartoon of Faith going to their headquarters at 575 Madison Avenue with me in the rear hanging on to her coattails. The ad was about to be released for the following week and I had my attorney send them a cease-and-desist letter to stop the publication. That got their attention. The next week, I was in their office with my attorney making significant changes (favorable to me, of course) to my Douglas Elliman's agreement.

Lesson learned: stand up for yourself when you have to.

Now we were in the new company. The industry had not heard much about Howard and Dotty at this point, since Howard was not from the real estate industry and Dotty was a relative unknown, although she came from a real estate brokerage firm called Merrill Lynch on Long Island.

Nevertheless, Faith was well known in New York City and heads turned when Faith and I moved to Douglas Elliman. Years prior, Howard Milstein, a major New York City landlord from one of the major real estate families, had owned Douglas Elliman. He had tried recruiting Faith many times and she almost went, but we had such a good thing going at Charlie's company that there was no need. Howard had a brother named Eddie and many times at our old firm I would say in a loud, high-pitched voice, "Eddie, where are you?" I would be standing at the window, looking north where their offices stood. Only Faith and I got the joke.

Later, I found out that Faith was fearful of making long-term commitments. She never married Jerry, her mate, whom she lived with for more than 30 years. And when it came time to negotiate with Douglas Elliman, she only negotiated a two-year agreement. To her credit, she negotiated a good deal with the new firm, paying for all the expenses.

Douglas Elliman was a residential firm and prior to our arrival, they had a small team of commercial brokers who were brothers, Gary and Rick Dana. Their father, Nick, who was retired by this time, had 50 years of service with Douglas Elliman. Howard asked if Faith wanted him to fire the brothers and Faith said that was not necessary.

Immediately, we designed all the signs and brochures and hired a public relations company: Howard Rubenstein. Our account executive was Filomena Fanelli. Who now has her own firm, Impact PR & Communications. She was a 22-year-old dynamo and she worked in tandem with Faith, orchestrating and delivering the marketing message—on our arrival at Douglas Elliman—perfectly. She stayed with us for the first few years. Once she decided to have a child, she left. That child today is a woman of 18 years of age. We then went and hired Alexander Marketing, the firm we had used at Garrick Aug. I always felt Linda Alexander was my business sister. She was brilliant and well-educated and corrected many of my writings, making sure my message was delivered properly.

She also knew all the press from the *New York Times*, the *Wall Street Journal*, the *New York Post*, the *Daily News*, and all the real estate trade newspapers and magazines. She was one-stop shopping when it came to the press, and always gave us wonderful results.

When we wanted to promote a project, she would do a fabulous job for us and for the property owner. When we wanted her to get the word out that we were representing a retailer or a property or that we had leased or sold a project, it always hit all the publications.

Debra Hazel, of Debra Hazel Communications, was our other publicist. She was keyed into the national market, and she knew all the top people at ICSC and the national press. She relocated to Las Vegas.

Linda and Debra were both the best in the business, and they kept us going nicely.

The firm was not giving us legal services, so they had us go to one of their legal vendors: a law firm that charged Douglas Elliman a hefty hourly number. Our legal bill in 2006 was $50,000 for commission and exclusive agency agreements. I felt that was a huge number. Other commercial real estate firms had a team of attorneys in-house that did all the agreements for the salespeople. Besides making sure Douglas Elliman got paid their commissions, our attorneys had to make sure the firm didn't have an exposure to being sued by other brokers, or the property owners for breaking the agreement for non-services.

While we were getting our feet wet at our new company, the investment banker that had bought Garrick Aug stopped paying our commissions. He owed Faith and me about $300,000 each. That was a lot of money in 2004. We had to sue him and Garrick Aug for non-payment. To make this story brief, on the day of the trial, no one from Garrick Aug showed up, so we won and got a default judgement. We never collected it, though, since at that point, there was no company left from which to collect. We later learned from the property owner where Garrick Aug was a tenant that they had never paid one month's rent. I always wondered: Who goes into a new business not even paying one month's rent? They were there nine (9) months before leaving voluntarily or by eviction. But then, there were $6 million of receivables in the street and the question is, did the new owners buy the company for $3 million just to get the receivables?

Other brokers didn't get paid either. The new owner had bought Garrick Aug, pledging the broker's commissions, which was the receivables, to pay Charlie his purchase price. If you know brokerage, you know that that money wasn't all of the buyers' to secure the loan, since the lion's share of each commission goes to the salesperson who made the deal. But somehow, they managed to pledge the brokers' portion of their commissions in addition to the company's portion, to borrow the money.

The first two years at Douglas Elliman went quickly and I did well in both years, not worrying about the expenses, because in Faith's deal the company paid for them. We were doing about twenty-five transactions a year with well- known retailers and property owners. I brought home $300,000 in both years, 2004 to 2006.

However, at the end of the second anniversary of the agreement, Faith got a letter cancelling the deal, and she was told that going forward, we must pay for the staff salaries and all the other expenses – or leave. The letter informed Faith that she had to have a check for them by the end of the week to pay the staff an amount of $6,000, or they were all going to be fired.

We were in shock.

I hired David Garelick, an attorney, to negotiate on my behalf. We met and we thought we were going to have an open dialogue with negotiations. Well, that's how far it went, but the other side gave a new meaning to the word, no.

They wanted us to pay for the first $500,000 in expenses before we would see any money. In anyone's book, that is a lot of money. In a business as competitive as commercial real estate, the norm is you get 50 to 70 percent of the commission, depending on your sales and seniority status. You take your share; the company takes its share; then the company pays the expenses. This deal did not mirror the norm of the industry at all.

We negotiated in good faith, no pun intended, but the company tried one more tactic. They stopped paying us. This is when I started shooting a steady stream of emails to Howard Lorber and Dotty Herman (the owners), David Fite (the CFO), Karen Chesleigh (head of human resources) who has since deceased, and Ron Miller (the Comptroller). None of the surviving C-Suite executives are with the company anymore. The company was out spending me on legal fees, as big corporations do, and I saw this could easily run into a six figure legal fee, and still I would not have a deal.

I ordered my attorney to stop negotiating. The company realized I wasn't going to sign any agreement to pay for the first $500,000 in expenses, and they brought down an independent contractors' agreement that I again refused to sign.

Lesson learned, One of the first rules of real estate is that you must trust the other party to do the deal.

But at this point, trust had left the room. Since I wasn't prepared to sign anything at this time, we had to set up a meeting with Howard and Dotty to try to get paid again. The tension was so high in my household, my wife's hair started falling out and she got rosacea on her nose.

In the time since Faith's agreement had not been renewed, I had learned a new word: reconciliation. In this context, it's the process of reviewing transactions and supporting documentation, and resolving any discrepancies that are discovered.

That was a good way to stall payment for about six months and that is what happened. When Dotty, Faith, Howard, and I met in Howard's office, I presented my four mounds of emails that had been sent. Not exaggerating: Howard's was ten inches in height, and the smallest pile was an inch and a half. I started the meeting telling them these were all the correspondences that had gone back and forth. There must have been about 400 pieces of paper, which I still have. I told them, "Howard, we want to get paid, you have been holding our commissions for six months" Howard said, "But you lost the company two million dollars last year." That was never proven, and I don't know where he got that number from, but he was a good negotiator and how could we fact check at that very moment and I kept quiet.

The night before this meeting I got a notion to check the New York State Licensing website to see if Howard's license was intact. Remember: Howard did not come from the real estate industry. His company owned Lorillard Tobacco, Nathan's Famous, and other companies.

The stacks of emails were on their side of the table. I said to them, "I amaze myself, these are all the letters I sent to you: Howard, Dotty, David, Karen and Ron. It's six months and we want to get paid."

Howard continued with the narrative that we lost money the previous year and how we must sign the new deal and he still must finish the reconciliation.

I asked Howard, "Do you have a real estate license?"

"Yes, I have a salesman's license."

"I checked the Department of State Real Estate Licensing website last night and you are right, you only have a salesman's license." I paused and went on: "With a salesman's license, you're not supposed to make any of these important management decisions. You are only supposed to play a passive role in the company." Howard kept quiet.

Later in the meeting, Dotty said to Howard, "He is fearless, he is not afraid." The tables completely turned, at least for that day. The meeting ended and Howard walked Faith and me to the elevator. I was furious, still having no money.

Howard said, "How much do you need now? I'll get you a check in a few days."

I didn't blink. I said, "Fifty thousand dollars." Howard said, "Okay."

In the elevator, Faith said she could not believe what had transpired. I told her, " Do you think he is taking us seriously?" Faith said, "Oh no, Howard's face went white when you told him about the license. He's taking you seriously."

It took two or three days, but I got a check for $50,000.

After this check arrived, we were back to square one. Payments never were timely and when they arrived, they came with a recollection spreadsheet of all the expenses that were charged to us: rent, phone, salaries, employee benefits, franchise fee, legal, marketing, education, and many more expenses.

This was the fifth real estate firm that I had worked for and never before had those deductions been taken out. I knew something was wrong. Howard Lorber was a certified public accountant by trade and he ran the business the way he wanted. Howard once told me he only made 10 percent off the residential side of the business. With Faith and I paying all the department expenses, he was making a clear 30 percent on the split and then another 45 percent from the expenses that the company was supposed to pick up, that Faith and I were paying. He was taking roughly 75 percent of all our deals.

I was taking home anywhere from 10 to 12 percent on a deal. Faith probably took the same amount. Remember, Howard wanted us to guarantee the first $500,000 in expenses, which I had never agreed to. Looking back on how we got paid, it turned out close to the deal he initially presented to us.

I always felt loyalty to Faith, as I did to Peter, Harry, Steve, John, and Howard, who were my former bosses. That is how I am wired. I tried to whisk Faith away and start our own firm. She would talk, but never budge.

Douglas Elliman gave her the title of Chairman of the Retail Department, which later became the norm in the industry. Nowadays, the real estate brokerage industry must have 50 or more chairpersons in New York City alone. Back then, she was part of a select few to have this title.

Years went by, and Howard got his way—taking all the expenses out. Faith and I always made deals. Once, we made one deal a week for an entire year.

One day, Faith leaned in and whispered that she'd heard from a reliable source that when Howard went to obtain his broker's license, he didn't take the test himself. Instead, according to the story, he sent someone else in his place—hoping to avoid recognition, as he was already one of the most powerful and recognizable figures in the industry. The tale goes that the stand-in was sent all the way to Albany, well outside Howard's usual territory, to keep things discreet.

Whether myth or fact, the truth may lie in a thumbprint—since every applicant is required to provide one before sitting for the exam.

Considering how Howard Lorber at Douglas Elliman was charging us for expenses, the arrangement felt entirely one-sided. We weren't even in a franchisee agreement—but even if we were, the standard royalty is typically just 3% to be paid to the house, the franchisor, with the franchisee covering most of the operational costs. Instead, we were paying out 30% while still covering all our own expenses. No matter how you look at it, we were being badly exploited.

Years later, as I prepare to publish this book, Howard has been accused of allegedly covering up for the Alexander twins—real estate agents at Douglas Elliman—who stand accused of drugging and raping 61 women. The FBI reportedly uncovered hours of video footage from multiple Alexander residences documenting these acts. Some of the recordings allegedly show other individuals present in the room, whose identities remain unknown.

The Alexander brothers claim the encounters were consensual, while all the women involved have firmly denied this. To date, only the twins and a third brother—also allegecly involved—have been indicted. All three are currently in prison awaiting trial. None of the other people in the room have been identified.

In addition to the criminal proceedings against the brothers, Howard now faces civil lawsuits from a ban of women, not sure of the number, who alleged he turned a blind eye to their misconduct.

At the time these alleged crimes were taking place, the Alexander twins were reportedly generating $1.8 billion in gross commissions. Plaintiffs argue that such staggering financial success may have motivated Howard's alleged silence and inaction. Another disturbing question lingers: who else was present during those acts?

Around that same time, Howard claimed to have retired from Douglas Elliman—shortly after selling his Vector Group holding company and its assets for $2.4 billion. He basically cashed out. However, some publications say he may have left for other reasons. Either way, he was planning to retire about three months later, at the end of 2024, but he left in September instead.

Several years ago, *The Miami Herald* interviewed the Alexander twins' father. He was quoted as sayirg, *"The boys are so close to Howard Lorber, that he could be considered their second father."* The question arises: just how close?

XXIII: INVESTING IN BROADWAY SHOWS

By now, I was looking for supplementary income. I received an email from Michael Rubenstein about investing in a new production of *Pippin*, the musical. I had seen the original *Pippin* with Ben Vereen. It was the role that made him famous. Naively, I thought Michael was part of Howard Rubenstein, the public relations house I mentioned earlier. I made a verbal commitment to invest and a few weeks later prior to signing, I told Michael how Faith and I came to Douglas Elliman, by going to his dad's company's 50ᵗʰ anniversary party years ago. That's when, Michael said, "My dad is not Howard, it's Samuel."

"Your dad is not Howard, of the public relations firm?"

"No, my dad worked in the garment center."

I said, "My mistake," and we both went quiet. I then said, "Michael, I like *Pippin*; I know it's going to do well and I am making the investment."

My wife and I were now Broadway investors. *Pippin* opened to glorious reviews. When we went to the opening party, we were hobnobbing with the comedian Martin Short and other celebs. We then invested in *Rocky*, the musical. At its opening night party, we met and had photos taken with Sylvester Stallone. We also met and chatted with Ramona Singer from *Housewives of New York*. I wondered whether she was considering Suzanne and me to be part of the series.

The next several years, we also invested in *Pippin*'s national tour, *An American in Paris,* and *On the Town.*

If a Broadway show breaks even, that's a huge event and it's a good reason for a big party. Most shows lose money, but the ones that hit can go on for years.

Either way, we had fun and it was a great experience. Suzanne and I learned a lot and Michael and I are still best friends.

Right around the time when we were investing in Broadway shows, we were getting invited to some grand parties with the stars. One was Bette Midler's Hullaween -New York Restoration party. It used to take place at the Waldorf Astoria before it got closed down to be converted into residential condos and a smaller hotel. We got dressed as Pirates as we hobnobbed with Sting, Yoko, Mariah Carey, Liz Smith, Patrick Demarchellier and other celebrities. (Photos are on the book website; see special link at the back of the book).

XXIV. BUYING THAT CONVERTIBLE; SIR ALEX FERGUSON

One year my wife and I decided that we wanted to buy a Mercedes convertible. Every week, I would call the salesman who had sold us our last car to find out that not only did they not have any in stock, but when he looked at the other Mercedes dealerships throughout the United States, none could be had.

We enjoyed going to the Hamptons in the summer and Labor Day was usually the last weekend that we would stay there.

Prior to getting on the highway, I told my wife, "Let's visit the Mercedes dealership in Southampton to select a color," since we had never decided on one. I wanted black or dark blue and she wanted white.

It was a formal process to check into that dealership. A receptionist takes all your information, name, phone, e-mail etc., and then asks whether there's a specific model you are looking for. We answered all of her questions and she led us to the seating area. We waited 10 minutes for our salesperson to arrive.

The salesmen arrived and graciously greeted us. I said to myself, "Here we go again. We are going to hear a lot of razzmatazz and 'Sorry, we have no convertibles in stock.'"

We told him the model we wanted and he said, "Oh, I think we just received a shipment." He looked further into his inventory and said,

"Yes, we just received an order of 12." My eyes widened. "What color are you interested in?" My wife chimed in, "White, with a black top and tan interior." He looked further into his book and told us, "We have one in the yard, but it's still in bubble wrap. No one has sat in it yet. Would you like to see it?"

I couldn't believe it; I immediately said, "yes," but my wife was suspicious. She suddenly crossed her arms, which is not a good sign in sales. That is usually an "I am not buying" sign.

We walked slowly to the car in the yard. I wanted to pick up the pace but dared not to show the salesmen how eager I was. Remember, I had already spent 50 hours tracking all the car dealers in the U.S. He had a box cutter and started to cut a line around the driver's door and then proceeded to the passenger's side to do the same.

My wife and I were in the car, and I found it had everything I had imagined and more. It had the sports package with all the bells and whistles. My hands were on a walnut burl steering wheel and gear shift knob. The seats were perforated so the conditioned air could cool you down on a hot summer day with a push of a button. It had a Harman Kardon surround-sound system. And it was a convertible. The color was the one that my wife liked, and by now I liked it too. I knew that the only one I must sell now was my wife. I stayed quiet.

We went back to the desk and discussed the price, down payment, and payment options. The salesperson refused twenty percent down and insisted that that was not the best way to buy the car. He suggested a lower down payment. He took my info, and told us we were approved. If we wanted the car, it was ours.

I immediately said, "Yes, we will take it." But my wife objected: "Aren't we being too hasty? Let's think about it for the week, and we will come back next weekend."

Only a few times in my life have I ever imagined overriding Suzanne, but this was one of them. I slammed my hand down on the salesman's desk and I announced, "We are not leaving here without the car."

The salesperson was rooting for me. I could hear him say under his breath, "Go get 'em, Joe." but he immediately chimed in, "Mr. Aquino, you can't take the car today, we still have to register the car and get you plates." I replied, "I know."

Suzanne said, "Aren't we being impulsive?"

I said softly, while holding her hand, "Sweetie, I have called my salesman at Manhattan Motors every week for the past 30 weeks. By no means are we being hasty and further, this car will be sold by the time we come back next weekend, so we must secure it now." She nodded and I knew I had closed my wife. As I was delivering the message to my wife, the salesman's head was nodding too, and he replied, "Yes, your husband is right, most likely this car will be gone by next week."

The following week, we picked up the car and I asked my salesperson to have a big red ribbon on the car to surprise my wife. When we arrived, there it was. The salesman took photos of us in front of the car and we drove off the lot.

Lesson learned: if you like it that much, just buy it.

Prior to this time, my wife and I had bought a beautiful apartment in the Manhattan House on Manhattan's Upper East Side, and we had been there for about eight years. Rachel Robinson, Jackie Robinson's widow, lived in our tower and we used to see each other on occasion. Rachel was active, and the last time I saw her, she was going on a safari in Africa with her daughter. I got a big smile out of Rachel when I told her I had been born during the week when Jackie and the Brooklyn Dodgers won the 1955 World Series.

I also lived in the same building with Sir Alex Ferguson, the former coach of the Manchester United soccer team. One time I was in an elevator with two couples. One couple got off on the second floor. I started chatting up the second one and from the man's accent, I thought he was British. He said, "Nah, I'm from Scotland."

I said, "You know Alex Ferguson lives in our tower."

He smiled and said, "I am Sir Alex Ferguson." I immediately apologized, telling him I knew nothing about soccer. But I told him how big of a fan my father-in-law was and that every time he came from Northern Ireland, "He would tell my wife that he was gonna knock on your door to say hello."

I told Sir Alex that my wife would say, "Don't you dare, Daddy."

Sir Alex laughed and said, "Oh, I would have welcomed your father-in-law and would have shared a pint with him." Once we got out of the elevator, he was kind enough to take a photo with me.

XXV. THE TRAVEL YEARS

I was always fascinated with Europe. I was up to date on my World War I and World War II history and I heard plenty of stories about Sicily and Italy, where my grandparents were from, when I was growing up. I was ready to start traveling to bring business back to New York City.

Faith scheduled a trip for me to go to London and she wrote a beautiful letter to all our English customers. Within a week, I had nineteen appointments in three days.

On the first two days, I met with shoe companies—Edward Green, Gina, and Emma Hope; with the best cufflink retailer, Pickett of London; and with jewelers like David Morris and Boodles. Finally, I visited some old cashmere houses, like Pringle. On my second day, I met with Joseph Wan, the CEO at Harvey Nichols. Faith called me when I was in the back of a cab. She said, "Guess who just called me?"

"The Queen of England?"

"No. Mohamed Al-Fayed's office, from Harrods. He wants to know if you're free tomorrow at 7:00 P.M. to come to his office."

I said, "Uhhhhhhhh," pretending that I might have another appointment. I said, "Let me check my schedule," and then said, "Yes, I am available—and if I hadn't been, I sure am now."

Faith gave me his details and the following day, I followed the instructions: go to the side street entrance, take the escalator up five flights. You will pass the Princess Diana and Dodi statue on the way up and on the fifth floor you'll find an unmarked door on which you will knock.

The next day, I headed for Harrods to meet the most impressive merchant on the planet. Harrods is one of the premier department stores, not only in Europe, but in the world.

I knocked on the door and the receptionist greeted me as though we were old friends. She showed me to one of the conference rooms, offered me tea, and said, "Mr. Al-Fayed will see you shortly."

I had brought with me plans for a 100,000-square-foot space that was available at the New Crystal's retail shops in Las Vegas. The property owner had planned to secure a mini department store. Joseph Wan had politely declined and I thought this would be perfect for Harrods. The plans were stacked 24 inches high off the table.

Mohamed Al Fayed entered the room and saw the stack of plans. He immediately opened his arms like the span of an eagle and said, "I'm not buying."

I opened my arms in reply, like his and said, "I am not selling," and we both laughed.

I gave him the pitch, anyway. He said, "Joe, no more retail for me."

I was dumbfounded. But I followed with, "Then what can I show you?" He said, "I want to buy class A office buildings." The next questions were, "What is your budget? What is the lowest price you would look at?" He said, "Don't show me anything less than half a billion dollars."

Then, amazingly, he started telling me about a project he was working on and said, "Come with me." In another room, he had a full-scale model of the Harrah's Hotel on the Las Vegas Strip—with the entire bottom portion of the building occupied by a Harrods store. He said, "I was working on this, but we are not going to do it." It would have been Harrods at Harrah's.

Now the meeting is over. Mr. Al-Fayed saw I had an old Harrods bag, and called out to his personal assistant, "Sarah, get Joe a new Harrods bag." As he was walking alongside me, Sarah handed him one. He handed it to me and took the old bag. He then went to his coffee table and put a tabletop book from Harrods into my new bag. Then, he went to his bookshelf and said, "You know I own the Ritz in Paris too," he put that book into my bag as well.

He then opened the front door and then stopped me abruptly. He put his right hand on my left shoulder and looked me dead in the eye and said slowly, in a serious low tone, "Now, Joe, you're going to come back tomorrow to Harrods and shop with your wife, right?"

I smiled, knowing I had just met one of the best salesman in the world, and said, "Of course Mr. Al Fayed, it would be my pleasure," Sure enough, the wife and I returned the next day and bought an entire duvet bed set and had it shipped back to our apartment in New York.

The following day, I had an appointment to meet Paul Kelly, the CEO of Selfridges, another top European department store.

I entered the side door of the building, this time, and I got clearance from the security guard. Suddenly, he said, "You're not going to meet Mr. Kelly with that bag, are you?" He was referring to my new bag that Mohamed Al Fayed had just given me, yesterday.

I said, "What can I do? Do you have a bag that I can put this in?"

"Let me see what I can find."

Ten minutes later, the guard returned, looking like he had been rummaging through a closet. He had a large Selfridge bag that was canary yellow, which was one of their corporate colors, but this one was badly used with grey duct tape all around it.

At this point, I was already 10 minutes late and I said, "It will do," I thanked him and put the Harrods bag into this huge yellow bag. I went onto the elevator thinking of the adage, "Does Macy's tell Gimbels?"

The meeting with Paul went well. He was an Irishman from the South and I told him I married an Irishwoman from the North, which helped to break the ice, but I was still in uncharted waters. It's rare that a European department store would come to America. I made my best pitch but Paul said "no" to the Crystals in Las Vegas.

I continued my travels. I started attending all the international luxury retail conferences around the world. After the London trip, I traveled to luxury summits and conferences in Venice, Singapore, São Paulo, Lausanne, Versailles, Rome, London, Marrakech, Mexico City, Florence, Venice, Beverly Hills, Paris, Madrid, Monaco, and Lisbon—and I brought back business.

I established some great friendships along the way. One was my dear friend, Riku Solapuro from Finland. Riku is one of the leading retail consultants and works for Icy Form. He represents many design and luxury brands in Northern Europe. if you have a luxury product you want to distribute in Northern Europe, you see Riku. We were so close that when he learned that his fiancée was having a baby, he called me first from Finland to tell me the good news. Riku went to everyone of the conferences that I attended including Tokyo, which I missed that year. He used to love to talk on the breaks. I would say, "Riku, we can talk later, now we gotta get cards!" Knowing that we had three days to meet all the top executives in the fashion industry.

In 2010 the Financial Times Luxury Summit was held at the Beverly Hills Hotel, located on Sunset Boulevard. I booked early and secured one of their famous bungalows: one-story structures by the pool that feature special interior designs. No two bungalows are alike. Name an old-time actor at the front desk, and you'll be told which bungalow that star stayed in.

The lineup of speakers for this conference included William Lauder of Lauder cosmetics, who recently passed away at 93 years old; Byran Lourd, the head of Hollywood's leading talent agency, CAA; Tamara

Mellon, who still owned Jimmy Choo; and Diane Von Furstenberg.

One afternoon before the summit started (I always arrived a couple of days early), I went to see a retail space with Anthony Palermo, a leading commercial real estate broker from the area. He showed me a space on Rodeo Drive and after that, we went for drinks at an outdoor restaurant at Two Rodeo Drive which is designed to look like it's situated on a street in Italy. We found we had a lot in common and before we parted, I invited him for lunch the following day at the Polo Lounge at my hotel.

The next day, I greeted Anthony in swim shorts and a t-shirt. It was obvious I was sunning and hobnobbing by the pool all day. The conference was going to start that evening with a roaring cocktail party.

Anthony mentioned that he had a customer, who was also a friend, who had been looking along Madison Avenue with no success: Michel Perrin of Perrin Handbags and Accessories. I said, "let's go meet him."

Anthony called Michel's store and was told, "Sure, come to the store; I am here."

While Anthony was getting his car from the valet, I slipped into my bungalow and put on a linen suit with linen shirt and tie and a nice pair of Bally slip-ons. When Anthony pulled up to the front door of the hotel, I was standing there with a briefcase in hand. I jumped into the car and Anthony said, "Wow, that was fast! Where's the phone booth?"

The meeting went well. I made a purchase and we discussed opportunities along Madison Avenue. It didn't take more than six weeks for me to find a store for Michel, and he had that store for 15 years. It was located at the base of the "old money" Carlyle Hotel on Madison Avenue and 76th Street.

In the same year, Faith and I brought two tenants to Anthony in Beverly Hills. We represented Joseph Schoenfelder, who had several brands of children's clothing stores, one was Monnalisa Kids—an Italian brand that has more than 40 stores, and also wholesales out of 800 doors—the location we secured for them was on Beverly Drive, and the other was LOL Kids Club which we brought to Sunset Boulevard.

In November 2013, I attended a conference that Suzy Menkes, the fashion icon, was hosting in Singapore with the International Herald Tribune. I took my wife with me. I had points built up on British Airways, so we flew first class. The ticket costs were $25,000, but I only had to pay for the taxes, which came to about $4,500. The trip was worth it.

On the return flight, one of the stewards said, "Mr. Aquino, where is your carry-on?"

I said "Above." He came back with a new bottle of wine.

He said, "I see you have been enjoying this brand, so please take this bottle with the compliments of British Airways."

The first leg of the trip was New York to London, where we stayed overnight at the Sofitel Hotel at the airport. The next morning, we took a cab to London and spent the day. It was near Christmas and we went to Harrods to shop. We then went to Fortnum and Mason for a fancy afternoon tea.

That evening we headed back to Heathrow Airport and flew 11 more hours to Singapore. We took a taxi from Singapore Changi airport to the W-Hotel where the event was being held. We always stay where the conference is, because you can meet someone of importance on the way to breakfast or by the elevator. The mission was to bring business back to New York or the U.S.A. and build relationships.

What they say about Singapore is true: it is small but immaculate. One of the places to go is the Marina Bay Sands: a development of three towers 55 stories high, connected on top by a huge platform the size of three (3) football fields. Some say the top looks like a big ark or a cruise ship. The buildings can be seen for miles, especially when you are flying into the airport. It's one amazing structure. The first third of the property sits on a 51-degree angle. During the first year of construction, the engineers had to put cantilever weights in the ground with cables connecting to the structure to keep it from falling over.

On the roof, you'll find a variety of restaurants, an infinity pool, and an assortment of discotheques. It is quite windy up there, especially at night, so be careful to hold on to something. The hotel has close to 2,600 rooms, a full convention center, and a shopping center at the base that has over one million square feet of space with more than 300 stores and plenty of restaurants.

The shopping center is laid out by use groups: a women's high-end clothing section; another section for premium men's shops; a beauty section; and so on. The development has a casino with approximately 1,000 tables and 1,400 slot machines.

I have been in the retail business most of my life and I had never seen anything like this.

Don't forget to visit Raffles Hotel: a colonial-style hotel by Armenian hoteliers, the Sarkies brothers, that opened in 1887. The hotel was named after British statesman Sir Thomas Stamford Raffles, the founder of colonial-era Singapore.

My wife was working for a Swiss company at the time and she had a colleague who took us to one of the finest restaurants there. My wife, over the years, did her share of foreign travel too, and many times I would join her. For this particular meal, her colleague ordered "dancing shrimp." Here's how they serve it to you: they wheel a cart with an open burner to your table, with its flame on high. They heat up a copper frying pan about 30 inches wide (which takes about five minutes), then they toss live shrimp into the oil-lined frying pan. As soon as the shrimp hit the pan, they start flying all over the place. Most of the time, one or two fall into your lap. Since you don't expect it, you immediately start to laugh and that's what Suzanne, my wife and I experienced that night with her colleague—who enjoyed our shock and amazement.

Suzy Menkes knew how to throw parties and how to attract the best fashion talent. Over the years, thanks to her, I met Tom Ford; members of the Pucci and Missoni family; Paul Smith; Ralph Lauren's son David; Oswald Boateng; and Diane Von Furstenberg to name a few.

One night, Suzy had a party at the Ocean Restaurant, within the Singapore aquarium. The glass connecting to the aquarium was 150 feet in width, 35 feet in height. On the other side of the glass were schools of tropical fish, hammerhead sharks, stingrays, manta rays, angelfish, goldfish, and other species too numerous to list.

On that trip, I met Umberto Angelioni from Caruso. He was originally the CEO of Brioni. He was thinking of opening a boutique in New York City. He also had a large store next to the Four Seasons Hotel in Milan on Via Gesú. He was planning on coming to New York for the week of Christmas to shop. I immediately saw the opportunity to cash in on this. We met back in New York and he chose to take a grand 10,000-square-foot gallery retail space called Spiegelman behind the Four Seasons Hotel on East 58th Street off Madison Avenue.

Mission accomplished!

I went to Florence and heard Leonardo Ferragamo, the CEO of Ferragamo, give a speech. Florence was his hometown, of which he was very proud. The Ferragamo Museum stores the family's historical artifacts. He gave his speech in a building a block away from it. He started by telling the audience how his family was celebrating the 100th Anniversary of his father Salvatore's moving to America. He went on to say that Salvatore landed at Ellis Island but finally found his way to Los

Angeles, where he became legendary, making shoes for a Hollywood clientèle. After the speech, I approached Mr. Ferragamo and told him that we had much in common, since my family was celebrating its 100th anniversary in America, too, also having landed at Ellis Island from Italy.

He said, "My family arrived April 7th, 1915."

"I think mine was sometime in March." I said, "Give me your card and when I go back home, I'll check the records."

One week later, I emailed him a photo of my family's ship, the *Re d'Italia* (King of Italy), which arrived the same day as his: April 7th, 1915. Ten minutes later, he emailed me a photo of his ship, *La Stampalia*, which had left from Naples while ours had left from Sicily. During this period, World War I was already in progress and Italy was about to enter it (on the side of the Allies, in August 1915). *La Stampalia* had stopped at Sicily on the way to the United States, and met my family's ship; together, they fled the terror of the War, arriving the same day at Ellis Island. The German U-boats were sinking cruise liners if they thought they were carrying munitions, so the ships had traveled together in case one was sunk.

On another trip, my wife and I went to a luxury conference in Marrakech, Morocco. Suzanne's brother lives in western Africa, married to a Ghanaian lady. They have two gorgeous children, a boy, and a girl. Unfortunately, we didn't get to visit them.

Marrakech has a 1500-year-old market known as a Souk, still open for business. One of the *Sex in the City* movies was filmed in Marrakech (only the audience was told they were in Abu Dhabi), so if you saw the movie, you have a feel of an open market, the people who sell there, and what we experienced.

When we traveled, we always got a local guide—and the guide would always stop us at a shop that he thought might interest us. Of course, he would have a deal with that shop, and would collect a commission on whatever was bought. The guide would ask us, maybe 30 minutes after we had come out of the store: how much did we spend?

This time, our guide took us to a merchant who sold rugs. The merchant was dressed like Aladdin, wearing balloon pants and a top with an eight-inch-wide black belt with a huge buckle. He had a turban on his head. The only thing he was missing was his sword. Having been a door-to-door salesman, I knew I was in for the show of my life.

He had two men taking rugs, out displaying them to Suzanne and me. He told us they were made by the local women who were part of the Moroccan Hand-Woven Rug Society.

It sounded good to me. The rugs were being displayed in all shapes and sizes, from 14 feet by 20, to eight feet by 11. Every time he showed me one, I would shake my head no. He would hold one hand on his belly, and when he spoke, he would raise the other hand, reaching upwards to the heavens, making all his points about all the carpets.

While his men were working the floor, he took out a silver pot, matching his Aladdin outfit, and poured mint tea, holding the teacup with his left hand close to his hip, while his right hand was above his head, the tea spouting out of the pot like a garden hose with no nozzle. The distance was four full feet, but not a drop missed the cup. The tea was sweet and delicious. His men kept bringing out carpets and I kept saying no. I knew Suzanne had just decorated our apartment in monotone colors and none of these mosaic rugs would work. Finally, I told him to stop. I informed him about our off-white apartment and offered him money for his showmanship and he said, "No, please I cannot take your money." He sat next to me like a friend and we chatted and enjoyed the tea.

He wanted to know all about us. I answered his questions and we had a nice visit.

When we left, we ran into a peddler who was selling a tin wine-bottle holder. My wife made the mistake of saying it was nice, and this peddler followed us into every store for the next 30 minutes. We were negotiating in dirhams, the currency of Morocco. I didn't know what the value of the currency was, but I knew how to negotiate and if a vendor sold me an item for half his original asking price, I thought I was getting a good deal. All my years of peddling, watch sales, health club sales, and negotiating with New York's top landlords came into play. I knew this fellow was in for a strong match. The only problem was, after 30 minutes, my wife screamed at me, "Give him the money or I am leaving you here and going back to the hotel."

I replied, "Whose side are you on anyway?" knowing that I had another good half-hour of stamina in me since I saw the guy was weakening. She said, "That is it," so I gave the guy his money. I was the owner of a tin crafted wine holder.

Back at the hotel, I put this prize possession on the mantle and asked myself, "What the hell did I just buy?"

Last night, the Four Seasons Hotel booked us at a traditional Moroccan restaurant where they gave us, I thought, the worst table in the house, by the door. I don't do it unpleasantly, but if I am not happy with service, I will say something. The wife hates when I complain, and warned me not to move us to another table, and I gave into her wishes.

The food arrived: stuffed peppers, just like my mom made 50 years ago. I could not believe it. Then I realized that Sicily, where my family is from, is not far from North Africa.

As we were finishing my meal, smoke rose from the floor, surrounding the grand staircase, and behind the smoke at the top of the staircase appeared 10 belly dancers, with lit candelabras on their heads. I realized that our "worst" table really was the best table in the house, in terms of the view we had. Two of the dancers approached our table, shaking their hips in my face for about 1C minutes while circling like a pack of Indians surrounding a stagecoach. I was getting red in the face. My wife was laughing, enjoying the moment.

It was done tastefully. My wife finally said, "Give them some money," and I apologized, not realizing why they stayed so long. I gave each of them $20, placing it in the silk pockets they wore at the top of their hips. Then they slowly moved tc the next table. Later that evening, I learned that Suzanne knew there was going to be a belly dancing show. Her Swiss colleague told her to make sure that she took me to a place like that.

The luxury summit, this time, was a star-studded event with the top leaders in the fashion industry.

We saw one Louis Vuitton store, which was the only sign of a luxury presence in the entire city. And we got to visit Pierre Cardin's Garden, which he had put into a trust prior to his passing to keep it freshly pruned for future generations to enjoy. Out of all the places we have been too, and there are plenty, we always enjoyed telling our stories about Marrakech to our friends.

One afternoon, our cab got stuck in Marrakech traffic, which consisted of being behind a camel with his rider and passengers. This was their rush hour and it moved as slow as the traffic on Fifth Avenue, midday.

It was November 2012, and I was invited to attend the International Herald Tribune Luxury Summit that took place in Rome. Prior to attending, when I was still in New York, I had gone to pitch the Regnum Christi Legionaries of Christ (RC), a Roman Catholic congregation of priests and men studying for the priesthood. Karen Dome, a colleague of mine who was one of the top real estate investment sales specialists in New York, joined me. The RC had bought the former 300-acre IBM corporate center in Thornwood, N.Y., years ago, as a study center, but now wanted to sell it.

At the meeting, it was clear that the RC had already made a choice as to its direction, telling us that they were close to their decision in selecting a real estate broker. I was pleased to learn that they were headquartered in Rome. I told them I would be there the following month and asked if it would be possible for one of their priests to give me a tour of Vatican City. To my delight, they said yes and in weeks to come, it was set that I would meet Fr. Thomas Montanaro on my last day in Rome, on Saturday morning, at 7:00 A.M., at St. Peter's Basilica. Suzanne wasn't going to accompany me this time.

I was booked at the Hotel Cavalieri, where the summit was to take place. I took a night flight, and when I arrived at the hotel, it was morning and daylight. Once in my room, I opened the curtains and saw St. Peter's Basilica less than a mile away. I had a clear view of the cupola. As large as the city of Rome was, what a coincidence that my hotel should be so close! I wondered, "What is God trying to tell me?" St. Peter's is the heart of Vatican City—and Vatican City is the heart of Christianity. The remains of St. Peter, the first Pope, are believed to be buried in the catacombs beneath the Basilica—which was built on this site in 329, at the command of Emperor Constantine, the first Christian Roman Emperor. Jesus said to Peter, "And I say unto thee, Thou art Peter, and upon this rock I will build my church; and the gates of Hell shall not prevail against it."

The summit was amazing. Many of the Italian fashion families, their executives, and the large luxury corporations came and joined the festivities. There was a black-tie event and they were all there from Valentino, Fendi, Prada, Ferragamo, Pucci, Furla, Della Valle from Tod's, Dolce and Gabbana, and many more. It was amazing: everyone was hugging and kissing each other on both cheeks, happy to see and be with each other. Most were Italian, and my being of Italian descent and having a grandmother whose name was Lucrezia (Borgia) Guarrasi, I knew the affection that these people had for each other and the thousands of years of their mutual heritage.

Saturday, when I would meet Father Montanaro, could not come quick enough and as usual, I had a pocket full of business cards from all the people I had met. I always enjoyed meeting new people. I took a cab and told the cab driver, "*Vorrei andare alla Città di Vaticano.*" (I'd like to go to Vatican City)

Father Montanaro and Brother Ryan were there waiting for me. After our greetings, Father Montanaro said, "Follow me." We were in St. Peter's, which is about the size of three football fields. All of a sudden, Father Montanaro came to a halt and told me to wait here and he would come back. While waiting for his return along with Brother Ryan, I was overwhelmed by the beauty of the inside of the basilica. The interior is filled with many masterpieces of Renaissance and Baroque art. At a distance I could see Michelangelo's *Pietà*; the Baldachin by Bernini over the main altar; the statue of St. Longinus at the crossing; the bronze cathedral of St. Peter in the apse.

Fr. Montanaro reappeared in full vestments, holding a chalice. Again, he said, "Follow me." Viewing the chalice, knowing the Eucharist was inside, I recognized that we were getting ready to celebrate Mass. We walked up to the main altar, where a staircase leads to the tombs and chapels below. I couldn't believe what was taking place. We went down several flights of marble stairs to the next level, where we encountered 12 chapels that circled a walkway in the center. We were not far from where Saint Peter's remains are said to be buried. Fr. Montanaro said, "I tried to reserve the chapel of Ireland in honor of your wife, but that was taken, so instead, I reserved the chapel of Europe, I hope you don't mind." On my left was a larger chapel, full of priests chanting hymns. It was a beautiful moment in my life.

The chapel of Europe was modest in size, maybe 250 square feet with three rows of pews. I dared not kneel in the first row. I took the second. Father Montanaro proceeded to celebrate Mass with Brother Ryan assisting him. The Roman Catholic Mass is a reenactment of Jesus' Passover supper with his Apostles: the Last Supper, when he knew what would happen the next day. The Eucharist, which we accept at Mass, is the literal body of Christ: one of the seven Sacraments of the Church.

I cried tears of joy, at the beauty of the Mass. Fr. Montanaro was reading from the Bible as Brother Ryan was turning the pages. I felt as though I had died and was at the gates of heaven and these two angels were going over the book of Joe, that was my life and they were determining whether or not I should enter into Heaven.

Once the Mass was over, I shared my sentiments with the priests. Then we faced an oil painting of Mother Mary—a 15th-century work by Bernini and we sang *Ave Maria* together.

After Mass, Fr. Montanaro changed back into his traditional robes and we proceeded to the Vatican Residences. The Vatican City looks like a 15th-century village, with cobbled streets. We entered a five- story stone building and took an elevator to the top floor. Inside, we found a huge round window with a clear view of the cupola of the Basilica.

We had a lovely breakfast, discussing serious topics like the right to life and human trafficking. After breakfast, Father Montanaro said, "Come on, we are going to tour the Vatican Museum." I couldn't believe it. I would have been satisfied with the visit up to that point.

When you are with these men, you don't have to wait on the one-hour line. Before I knew it, we were inside looking at all the works of art. As we were walking and viewing the paintings, Fr. Montanaro was telling me, "This one is Caravaggio, that one is Bernini, and over there is Raphael." He was also saying, "The person in that painting is Saint Matthew, that one over there is John the Baptist, and that other painting over there is Saint James. Oh, and by the way, through that window, you can see the Pope's summer residence."

We finally came to the Sistine Chapel, where Michelangelo painted the famous scenes from the Book of Genesis on the ceiling and the walls. I'd been there twice before, once with my sister and then with my wife, but always welcomed another visit. Fr. Montanaro asked, "Have you been to the Room of Tears? I said, "No, what is that? " He replied, "That is where the newly elected Pope goes."

, "He leaves this room where the College of Cardinals has just elected him. Waiting for the new Pope in that room are three vestments. He tries them on and wears the one that fits the best and then he sits down and signs the document making him officially the Pope. Then the Cardinals hand him the keys to Vatican City. As he sits, he contemplates what words he will first say to his flock—and it's called the Room of Tears because the new Pope usually sheds tears of joy."

When I entered the room, I saw it was of modest size, maybe 150 square feet. It is specially designed for the Pope to sit, contemplate, and then to go meet his flock for the first of many times. The small desk and chair look like they could be found in a child's school classroom. The desk faces the door, through which you can see the entire Sistine Chapel. Behind the desk is a small lancet window. This is a high narrow stained-glass window with a point on top that faces in the direction of heaven. On the wooden desk the security guard had put down the set of keys he had used to open the door; they looked like the type of keys used centuries ago, with a large iron ring holding them. For me, they symbolized the keys of Vatican City the Pope is given on the day of his election. Directly behind where the Pope sits, a crucifix hangs on the wall to the left of the window. To the right is a corridor, but I dared not walk in that direction. That's the route the Pope takes to the balcony to meet his flock for the first time.

Earlier in the book, I mentioned how I always beat the crowds and how I would show up to a restaurant before it got packed—and how I would get to a deal before my competition. Today was no different. I thought the next time this room was to be used would be 10 to 20 years from then, but that was not the case. Only a few months later, on February 28, 2013, Pope Benedict XVI stepped down.

I was sitting at my desk, back home in New York, on March 13, looking at the screen of my computer. I was watching www.msn.com's landing page—and I saw white smoke coming out of the smokestack of the Sistine Chapel, which meant a new Pope had been elected. When black smoke comes out, that means the Cardinals will have to take another ballot—no candidate having yet won a two-thirds majority. At first, I thought I was watching a former Pope being elected, and then I realized I was watching in real time. I called my assistant and told her to hold my calls for the rest of the day. In the next several hours, I saw two oompah bands march out individually and play; then, after a further long wait, Pope Francis appeared.

Jorge Mario Bergoglio, Cardinal just a few hours ago, was now standing humbly as the new Pope in front of 20,000 people under his balcony in St. Peter's Square. He had just left that tiny Room of Tears and walked down the long corridor.

His first words were, *"Buonasera!"* It was a beautiful moment. It was fitting that I should witness this magnificent event, but I never see things like this as a coincidence. It was meant for me to be in my office that day, rather than on an appointment. By the way, I didn't get the assignment for Thornwood, but I knew I got much more.

When you travel and go to these events, you eat well and below are some of the dishes we had along the way...

XXVI. THE GUARRASI FAMILY

My maternal grandparents' name was Guarrasi. They left Palermo on March 23, 1915, and arrived at Ellis Island on April 7. My grandparents' names were Giuseppe and Lucrezia. They brought their sons, my uncles: Tommaso, Pietro, Vincenzo, and Giuseppe. My grandfather's sister was already established in Brooklyn. Her name was Antonia. My mother was named after her. She already owned a building with a salumeria that she operated downstairs on 21st Street, between Third and Fourth Avenues. Everyone called her Ah-Zia. Years later I learned that that came from "*la zia*": the aunt. I understand she sponsored all of my family who arrived from Alcamo, Sicily.

My grandparents had 14 children. Two sets of twins died at birth. Uncle Vincent got killed as a boy, crossing Fourth Avenue, by a truck owned by the American Can Trucking Corp.

Years ago, two of my cousins traveled to Sicily on a tour to find their roots. One day, they got an English-speaking driver, left the tour and went to see if they could meet any relatives in our hometown. They entered a cafe in the main square of the family's original home town, and the driver asked if there were any Guarrasi's in town. One man said, "I went to school with one," and immediately got him on the phone.

His name was Paolo and he spoke English. He said to my cousins, "Why didn't you let me know you were coming? I would have met you. I am out of town today." Then he went on to tell them that they would have to go to the Palazzo di Guarrasi, a 15th-century 15-room *palazzo* located on Via Guarrasi across from the church. "Ask for Giuseppina. She is the new owner."

That afternoon, Robert and Phillip knocked on the door of that house, with their driver's licenses in hand, ready to show Giuseppina that they were Guarrasi. She was warm and welcoming and immediately invited them into the house.

Giuseppina went on to tell them that the building had stood derelict for decades while she and her family lived directly across the street. She always told her parents that one day when she got older, she was going to buy the property and totally restore it, which she did. She made the property a condominium, selling the rear portion of the house, and keeping the front portion for herself. The property sat on a blockfront and had two corners facing two separate streets.

When the brothers referred to themselves as "Italian," Giuseppina stopped them and said, "We are not Italians. We are Sicilians and this is Sicily." I knew from my readings, Sicily was like a beautiful woman that everyone conquered over the centuries, some of the people who conquered her or settled there were Normans, Byzantines, Phoenicians, Swabs, Arabs, French, Spaniards, Vikings, Greeks—and the Bourbon royal family.

Finally, around 1860, Giuseppe Garibaldi, along with others, conquered Sicily and Naples and brought them into the unified Kingdom of Italy. Before this, Italy had consisted of many principalities. Vittorio Emanuele II di Savoia, King of Sardinia, became the first King of Italy.

I know from family stories that Grandma was a schoolteacher and grandfather owned a quarry that mined marble. Grandma had a staff and always rode in a horse and carriage. It is just possible that Giuseppina's palazzo was my grandparent's residence. One day, I will go there myself and check the records at their City Hall.

My grandparents left this all behind and never returned to their small town, because World War I broke out and Italy was about to enter it. They fled to America for their safety. That was a horrific war that took the lives of millions, and conceivably my grandfather would not have survived to have such a huge, beautiful family if he had stayed in Sicily.

Grandma Lucrezia had a famous maiden name, Borgia. That was that of Alexander VI, the Borgia Pope. He was Spanish and from Valencia. Rodrigo Borja took his mother's maiden name Borja (italianized to Borgia). Rodrigo's uncle was Pope Callixtus III—which is probably why Rodrigo became Vice Chancellor of the Catholic Church at a very early age. He served under four Popes—then became Pope Alexander VI.

Pope Callixtus is the Pope who drew the line in South America, leaving Brazil to Portugal and all the rest to Spain.

Pope Alexander had four children by one of his mistresses, Vanozza dei Cattanei: three boys and a girl, Lucrezia. The boys came to no good end, but Lucrezia bore at least seven children, perhaps eight. The first is said to have been fathered by her brother Cesare. The others were beared by her third and last husband, Alfonso D'este; her brother-in-law, Francesco II Gonzaga; and a couple of other lovers. She died at the age of 39, shortly after the death of her daughter.

Lucrezia Borgia, which my grandmother was named after, was known for her blonde hair, her prettiness, agreeable personality, and many of the good works she did for the people.

Pope Alexander had also had other children by other women. Somehow at least one of them got to Sicily.

When I had to identify my grandparents departure and arrival date from Palermo, Sicily to Ellis Island, New York, it was simple. Grandmother had her name simply spelled out on both ship records, Lucrezia (Borgia) Guarrasi.

CHAPTER XXVII — BUCCELLATI

For years, we represented Buccellati, the storied 100-year-old Italian jeweler with more than 60 stores worldwide. They're most famous for their iconic shop at the entrance of the Ponte Vecchio Bridge in Florence.

In New York, they had leased a building at 48 East 57th Street for many years, with several years still left on their lease. At the time, Harry Macklowe — a major developer in New York City — was assembling a development site around them in partnership with CIM, a Los Angeles-based developer founded by two former Israeli paratroopers. Harry wanted Buccellati's property as part of the assemblage and had been negotiating directly with them for years. But the two sides couldn't agree on a buyout price.

Faith and I met with one of the paratroopers, and — to no one's surprise — he was a tough negotiator. He told us plainly that he planned to build around Buccellati, and the disruption from construction would put them out of business.

He wasn't entirely wrong. When construction begins next door, scaffolding goes up over your door and windows, trucks clog the street delivering materials, and crews come and go at all hours — not ideal for a luxury jeweler.

Out of nowhere, I slammed my hand on the table, hard enough that the room seemed to vibrate. Everyone was stunned. I said:

"These are Italians. Over the centuries, they've been invaded at every border. You might think you can put them out of business, but let me tell you — before they even put the key in the door each day, they make $2 million a year just visiting their clients' homes and selling jewelry privately. And your brokers are probably telling you that the extra 20 feet you'd gain on 57th Street from their building won't matter. But every foot you move closer to Fifth Avenue makes your project more valuable. Trust me — in two years, you'll thank me for convincing you to take their deal."

He looked at me and said, *"How much do you want?"* I named a figure that was double his last offer. He said, *"Okay. I'll call you tomorrow at 9:00 A.M. with my decision."*

The next morning, he called. His offer wasn't quite double — but it was close. Buccellati accepted, agreeing to vacate once the funds were delivered.

Shortly after, we completed two additional deals with Buccellati — one relocating them to Madison Avenue, and another in Chicago. The Chicago deal was done in collaboration with one of our Secret Broker Society members, the exceptional Gwen Callans of Atlas Partners. Together, we secured a lease for Buccellati at 62 East Oak Street.

That same year, we also opened another store in Chicago at 900 North Michigan Avenue for another of our luxury clients, Sermoneta Gloves, also with Gwen. Known for their handmade Italian gloves, Sermoneta offers a dazzling palette of vibrant primary colors alongside elegant natural tones. Faith and I originally brought them to the U.S. market, opening their first store at 609 Madison Avenue and 58th Street.

Sermoneta is a family-owned business of Roman Jews, with a lineage that traces back over 3,000 years in Rome. In fact, their temple stands directly across from St. Peter's Basilica in Vatican City.

XXVIII. WHO WAS FAITH HOPE CONSOLO?

She was a fierce competitor. She would often say, "I bend, but never break." But if you knew her soft side, you would find the kindest and most generous person in the world.

Since we both lost our parents at an early age, and were orphans, we had a bond like no other in the industry. We constantly had each other's backs. We would take turns in our roles relative to each other. One day, I could be her father, or she, my mother. On another day, we could be brother and sister, but either way, we were an unbreakable team.

Faith had a children's charity in the Bronx in which she loved to participate and every year before Christmas, she would fill up several cars with gifts and bring them up to the children. Judy Sahagian, also known as Judy Networks, used to assist her and she could vouch for how charitable Faith was.

She was also involved in Women in Need and she got me involved in that charity as well. This charity was close to her heart because there was a period when she was on her own, without shelter, after her break-up with her first husband.

She was also active in the Association of Real Estate Women (AREW), which eventually merged into Commercial Real Estate Women (CREW). During her tenure, she was elected President and achieved a record year for new membership. She was passionate about supporting the organization and empowering women to advance their careers in real estate through networking and mentorship.

Faith loved Christmas and she spent Christmas Eve with my family, which consisted of my sister and her husband and of course my wife. Her partner, Jerry, seldom participated. She would show up on Christmas Eve with the most lavish gifts, well thought out, for each person and everyone valued her generosity. She would also send a case of champagne to my residence, and we managed to finish most of it at the party.

Some of her staff loved her too. She had many assistants over the years. One was Yvette DeJesus, who finally became a teacher and cried the day she left Faith. Nancy Rondon, another assistant, is now a tremendously successful residential broker in the Bronx. She says she likes to channel Faith's energy through her marketing and she does a fabulous job on social media. She is very easy to find if you need a good broker for her market including Connecticut and Northern Manhattan.

For years, on days when we were in the office together, we would order lunch in, from a place called Delectica. When it was time for lunch, we would yell out at a high pitch, "Delectica," and we would both laugh. We always ordered the same thing— a tuna sandwich on pita bread, which we would share. That stopped once we went to Douglas Elliman.

The offices we had at Douglas Elliman had previously belonged to Howard Milstein, the developer and landlord, and they were huge. The Milstein family is one of the bigger New York City real estate families. Faith's corner office must have been 1,000 square feet. It was nicely decorated with custom shelves, mirrors, sofa, chairs, a cocktail table with coffee table books, and accessories and a big screen TV which she always watched Bloomberg. All her awards were lined up on a 40-foot ledge with photos in silver frames displaying celebrities, friends, and loved ones.

Faith was the darling of the press and we all learned from her, including Howard and Dotty. Faith was quoted in the papers almost daily—usually in the *Wall Street Journal,* the *New York Times,* the *New York Post,* the *Daily News, Women's Wear Daily,* and all of the real estate trade papers. We had two publicists, one regional and the other national, and Faith knew how to use them. She led them daily in her mission to get her name out, along with Douglas Elliman's and whichever property owners or retailer we were representing.

Faith regularly appeared on Neil Cavuto's TV show on Fox News. She was developing her own TV series called The Faithful Fashionista that promoted our retailers and Douglas Elliman.

When the press would call, Faith's staff was trained to say; "Are you on deadline?"

Remember, when Faith joined Douglas Elliman, no one knew Howard and Dotty. But, now with the Faith press machine, they were becoming well known. Companies like Apple, Microsoft, and automobile companies would pay millions to advertising companies to get this type of coverage. Douglas Elliman was getting it for free.

Faith even managed to get a lead part in an Off- Broadway Show called *Luscious Lucille,* which played for one evening to a packed house.

The property owners and retailers loved her. Everybody got a bottle of champagne and a thank you note when the deal got done. She was well respected and trusted and many shared their most intimate secrets with her. She was brilliant and a master planner.

Many people said, "Yes, Faith was tough, but there was something everybody liked about her." She had irresistible charm and style. She had a good fashion sense, an award-winning smile, a great personality, and she could be warm and funny. She enjoyed life, daily. I never heard a complaint.

She wasn't a big fan of brokers — and the feeling was mutual. They would do whatever they could to tarnish her image. Remember, brokerage is an extremely competitive business.

When *The Real Deal* launched their publication, they allowed readers to post anonymous comments on articles. It was brutal what they let happen. People wrote the most awful, untruthful things about Faith.

This went on for nearly two years, until *The Real Deal* had firmly established itself in the industry. Only then did they finally put a stop to it.

No one knew how much Faith was worth, but she did appear to have significant assets, and naturally people wondered whom she would leave her money to, when her time came. Some people thought it might be me.

I never once asked Faith what she was worth, and she always bragged about how she could trust me with her money. She often told me that she would leave her share of the commissions to me.

I never thought about the subject further or asked anything of her. I never looked at Faith as a dollar bill.

Faith had once owned her own interior design firm, and it had failed. Ever since, she had been afraid to go out on her own. When Robert Futterman opened his own firm, the market welcomed him, and when Garrick Aug imploded, I think the market was expecting the same from Faith. Instead, she and I went to Douglas Elliman.

XXIX. MY RELATIONSHIP WITH HOWARD

In 2014, I brought Williamson Picket Gross to Howard Lorber, and he eventually did a deal with them. He absorbed an entire office leasing company and integrated them into the firm. At the time, the company policy stated that when you introduced a salesperson to the firm, you would receive a finder's fee. I was told by Ester Muller that it was supposed to be $15,000 per person—though this wasn't outlined in the company manual. Supposedly, that's what Ester received when she brought Faith and me into the company.

I wrote to Howard, "...if the company still has a policy of paying a broker a referral fee, I would like to receive mine for getting them interested in bringing their group here."

Howard replied, "I'm happy to pay you five percent of the purchase price."

I responded, "Faith is my partner on the WPG referral. We will share the referral percentage fee 50-50."

Howard came back with, "They came as commission brokers. Their company was over. Paid nothing."

I replied, "Hysterical! Why would I agree to take nothing? Then we have to go to the standard Douglas Elliman referral fee, which is in effect."

Nothing ever came of it.

Another time, I secured Douglas Elliman, an exclusive agency to sell over 100 new residential units at a superstructure in Long Island City—a project called L-Haus. Faith and I had represented the Stahl Organization for years. Douglas Elliman was relatively new to Long Island City, but I convinced them to give Stahl the assignment. Two-bedroom units were selling for $775,000 back in 2010. The total sellout of the building reached about $100 million, which translated to $5 to $6 million in commissions.

Howard gave me a pittance—$25,000—as a referral fee, which I split with Faith. Collecting that money wasn't easy either. It took months. I always felt that the referral fee should have been well into six figures. But not with Howard.

Eventually, I stopped trying to build Douglas Elliman—despite how much my hard work was appreciated—because I never felt properly rewarded. It brought me back to one of the first lessons I learned, which I share in this book: *Schnorrer!*

XXX. DECIDING TO SUE

1. Carrying the Load

By 2014, Faith and I were covering the full cost of running our division at Douglas Elliman—including all of the employees assigned to us. We paid for their salaries, their health benefits, their vacation time—everything, 100 percent. These were Douglas Elliman employees, but the firm made no financial contribution to their compensation or benefits. All of it came out of our commissions which I felt was wrong.

In addition to paying our team—which included five or six staffers and two publicists—we were also covering the cost of a high-end law firm, rent, phones, office supplies, PR expenses, subscriptions, even a franchise fee and other overhead that I believed should have been handled by the company like weekly flowers on the reception desk.

2. Seeking Legal Advice

Frustrated, I consulted Cindy Salvo, a childhood friend from my Brooklyn days. We met at the 40th Anniversary reunion of Midwood High School that I should have gone to, if I didn't enroll In Aviation High School. She was a licensed attorney in New York and New Jersey. I explained that if I was footing the bill for Douglas Elliman's staff, then I was functioning more like an employer than an independent contractor—and that I should be treated accordingly.

Cindy agreed. I also explained that I had never consented, verbally or in writing, to all of the deductions being taken from my commissions. I had submitted numerous memos raising objections and had face-to face meetings with the Douglas Elliman C-Suite executives over the years. Cindy believed we had a viable claim and suggested we file in federal court, which typically moves more swiftly than New York State court.

3. The Federal Filing

We filed a nine-page complaint in federal court. Among the claims were violations of the Fair Labor Standards Act, New York Labor Law Article 6 (unlawful deductions), and Article 19 (minimum wage protections). The complaint alleged that Douglas Elliman had improperly deducted a wide range of expenses from my commissions, including (but not limited to):

◊ Employee salaries
◊ Secretarial and receptionist support
◊ Training and educational programs
◊ Public relations and promotions
◊ Car services and travel
◊ Membership dues and subscriptions
◊ Legal and consulting fees
◊ Franchise fees
◊ Advertising and photography
◊ Temporary employees
◊ Miscellaneous operating costs

4. Telling Faith

Faith and I were at JFK, sitting in a restaurant, waiting to board our flight to Las Vegas for the ICSC conference. I told her I was filing the lawsuit against Douglas Elliman—and asked if she wanted to join me.

"What, are you crazy?" she said.

"No," I answered. "I'm just tired of coming home with hardly anything."

Instead of coming home with 35% each, the split of 70% that we shared, we were coming home with 10-12% each.

That was the beginning of my effort to pull her away from the firm.

5. From Federal to State Court

From the outset, the Magistrate in Federal Court began stalling, my attorney only met the judge once. Rather than moving the case forward, he repeatedly called meetings with my attorney. Every time they met, she came back more disheartened. He never ruled on anything substantial—he just kept her in conversation, slowly wearing her down.

Eventually, after about a year, he told her, "I believe your case doesn't belong here. You should file in the New York State Supreme Court instead."

He didn't dismiss the case—he simply persuaded her to walk away. In my view, he persuaded her to leave. Which means if I agreed, I would not get my day in Federal Court.

I didn't understand why we couldn't get our day in Federal Court. But she appeared frustrated and I believed she started to lose interest and

I was convinced there was no way forward. I advised her that I agreed and told her, "Ok, let's refile in State Court."

6. Faith's Name Appears

When the new Supreme Court complaint was filed, it went through without my signature — something I later learned is allowed in New York if the attorney is from out of state. But when I finally reviewed the filed version, I was stunned to see that Faith's name had been included, along with claims that she had taken some expenses from my commissions. I was furious — and by then, it was too late to remove her name.

I immediately called Cindy and demanded, *"Why is Faith in here? We're not suing her."*

The draft she had originally sent me was so heavily black- and red-lined it was almost impossible to decipher. I had asked her to send me a clean version, but I didn't actually see one until after it had already been filed.

Including Faith had never been part of the plan — and it only made an already difficult situation even more complicated.

7. Dismissed from the Firm

Shortly after the second complaint was filed, with Faith's name in it, about one week to be exact, Steven James, then-President of Douglas Elliman, came into my office.

"Okay, Joe. You have to leave now."

"What do you mean?" I asked.

"You know what I mean. You can't stay. We'll pack your things and send them to your home."

I quickly grabbed what I could. Then I walked into Faith's office to say goodbye. At first, I was hiding in a back room, but I soon realized this was really happening and I was being fired. She offered a few words. It was clear: our 26-year partnership had ended. She had already brought back Harry, her first partner from decades earlier.

I had always allowed Faith to be the face of our team. That had made her happy. Now the partnership is truly over.

Arthur Maglio, a broker we had hired, helped me to the curb with four shopping bags of my personal belongings that I grabbed quickly, and I got into a cab. You can imagine, I was devastated.

8. The Article Drops

Just 30 minutes after I was escorted from the office, *The Real Deal* published a story about the lawsuit. I felt the timing was no coincidence. I was convinced no one could have written that story so quickly and I believe I was right.

The headline read:

> "Faith Hope Consolo's lavish spending habits are eating up the lieutenant's commissions, he claims in a new lawsuit against Douglas Elliman."

The article continued:

> "Joseph Aquino, right-hand man to self-styled 'Queen of Retail' Consolo, is suing the brokerage, alleging it improperly deducted over $1 million of his commissions to pay for Consolo's extravagant personal expenses."

I had never spoken to the press. The article felt planted. From my perspective, the way Faith's expenses were framed didn't reflect reality. I was suing Douglas Elliman over the expenses they took from me to operate the department—but the story twisted it into something else, making it seem as if the only reason they took those expenses was to cover Faith's personal spending.

Faith texted me just ten minutes after the article came out: *"We are no longer family."*

I was crushed. It was a divorce. I was no longer in partnership with Faith—the person I had considered my best friend, my mentor from the very beginning, and my partner in hundreds upon hundreds of deals. Together we had represented the top luxury retailers and property owners in the world, and worked on major consultancy projects. To lose her was devastating.

9. Commissions and Confrontations

After being forced out, I expected to finally receive my commissions directly. But my attorney later discovered that some commission sheets had been initialed by Faith, suggesting she had claimed both her share and mine. I was shown a split sheet by my attorney and asked to confirm if those were her initials. I said, "Yes, but I still can't believe it."

At this point, my attorney advised: "You may have to add her to the suit. If you don't, it could weaken your case."

I resisted—but weeks later with none of my money coming in, I eventually conceded. "File it," I said.

10. The Deposition

Douglas Elliman continued to use **Kasowitz Benson Torres**, the powerhouse law firm known for representing high-profile clients — and for getting results, at a very steep cost. I was told that when Howard Lorber was close to Trump and doing business with him through

Douglas Elliman, he relied on **Kasowitz Benson Torres** which Wikipedia even lists as Trump's personal attorney at the time. I also heard Howard Lorber and he were good friends. (This was before Trump became President.) One of the high-profile cases **Kasowitz Benson Torres** handled for Trump was during the Russian collusion investigation.

Howard Lorber used **Kasowitz Benson Torres** because of that connection. And I do believe they were close, but ever since Trump 1.0 and Trump 2.0, you don't see or hear Howard Lorber associated with him. He never landed a Cabinet position, an ambassadorship, or any ancillary role in either administration.

It always struck me that Lorber must have really felt threatened by me to hire such a high-powered, high-priced law firm as **Kasowitz Benson Torres**.

Maybe I even played a role in cooling their relationship. I had written to Trump's daughter, Ivanka, detailing all the shenanigans going on behind the scenes at Douglas Elliman during that period — and let's not forget, Trump was quite fond of Faith.

Then, Howard Lorber may have influenced the Douglas Elliman board to hire **Kasowitz Benson Torres** yet again — this time to conduct an internal investigation into whether the firm had any dealings in looking the other way with the Alexander twins. But seemingly shortly thereafter the board relieved them of their duties — allegedly due to concerns over Howard Lorber's close ties to the firm.

And here's the irony: Douglas Elliman's longtime house counsel Ken Haber went into semi-retirement, and who replaced him? Deva Roberts — an attorney who had previously worked at **Kasowitz Benson Torres**.

Oh, and by the way — shortly afterward, Howard Lorber quietly stepped down from his position, claiming he was retiring. His private jet was taken back by the firm not long after.

Was the installation of Ms. Deva Roberts just another example of the fox guarding the henhouse?

When I arrived for my deposition, a camera was already set up. The conference table stretched 25 feet. I sat alone while two attorneys questioned me for hours. I was miked up and I felt like a Senator at one of those Congressional hearings., It felt less like a deposition and more like an interrogation.

They pushed me hard—grilling me on the expenses in question, the allegations, and my relationship with Faith, my agreement. It was a grueling day, starting early in the morning and running straight through to closing. Every question was recorded on camera, and a stenographer typed every word. We only broke for lunch and the occasional bathroom break.

With all the relentless questioning, I held my ground.

They came close to breaking me. But they didn't.

Faith, on the other hand, never showed up for her deposition. It was postponed several times—and ultimately, it never happened.

11. REBNY's Response

Hoping to find some form of support, I reached out to the President of the Real Estate Board of New York. I laid out my story in detail, describing the years of toxic behavior that Faith and I had endured.

Weeks later, I finally got a response — but not from him. Someone from his office wrote: *"REBNY does not get involved in disputes once a lawsuit has been filed between members."*

I was stunned. I had turned to the largest landlord and broker organization in our industry for help, and after everything I'd been through, all I got was a closed door and silence.

You may be asking yourself: *Why didn't they just leave?*

Believe me — we tried. But it felt like we were fighting against three glass walls.

First, whenever we approached other firms and sat down with their top people, we were face-to-face with our own direct competitors, asking to join them. Many of them outright disdained us.

Secondly, Faith's visibility worked against us. Even before he became President, Donald Trump once told her: *"Faith, you get more press than me."* She was more visible than the very people running these big firms — and they didn't want her stealing their thunder. Twice we went to these companies. The first time together, and then by myself years later when I was on my own. No one threw us a liferaft.

And lastly, the industry was so insular, so small, that I always suspected someone was quietly sabotaging us. I could almost hear the whispers: *"Oh sure, they're good — but I lose money on them every year because they run high on expenses."*

You may also be asking: *Why didn't Douglas Elliman just fire me while the case was in Federal Court?*

The answer is simple. Kasowitz Benson Torres, Douglas Elliman's attorney, wanted all the labor charges dismissed quietly, without trial. If I had won in Federal Court, it would have blown the lid off the industry. I believe it would have forced real, meaningful change on the wrongdoers — changes that would have benefited every real estate salesperson out there.

Deep down, I've always believed someone "dropped a dime" on the judge. That's why I think the Magistrate never wanted the case to go to trial.

That's just my opinion, of course.

XXXI. MY STENTS

One day, I was taking a long walk in Central Park and I felt a strange tingling in my fingers. I immediately scheduled an appointment to see my cardiologist. The next day, he took a stress test with contrast. This is where they pump your arteries and heart with a non-toxic dye and take X-rays of your chest. The following day, my doctor called and announced that I needed two stents and "When can you come in?"

Being the great negotiator that I am, I pushed for the end of the week. He told me one of my arteries was fully closed and the other one was 47 percent clogged. I won the battle. Once the call ended, I thought I better call him back and ask him how many arteries my heart has. I got the doctor back on the phone and he said, "Three."

"Your middle one is totally closed," he said. "They call this the widow artery, which is self-explanatory. The right artery is 47 percent clogged. As the major arteries close, the smaller arteries expand to keep the blood flowing to the heart."

My voice must have raised two octaves. I told him, "I can come right over to have the procedure done."

"I can't do that. I must get the hospital on board—and find you a surgeon."

"What about tomorrow?" The call ended shortly thereafter.

He called back several hours later, "The best I could get was the upcoming Thursday."

I realized that if I had been working diligently at my old desk with Faith, I might have not noticed the numbness in my fingers. I could have had a major heart attack and died in my office or on the subway. I became thankful that I had been home for the past few months. My body had had several months to rest prior to the operation. My nature has always been to look at the bright side.

It took two separate procedures to have my stents done. The first one took about two hours and the surgeon was able to open the closed artery fully.

If he had not, they would have had to crack open my chest and do a bypass. A month later I went back to do the second one, and it took a much shorter time. Before both procedures, as I was strapped to the gurney, I remembered that I had lost both my parents from heart attacks. I thought it was my turn, and feared I was not going to wake up after the operation. As you see, I did.

XXXII. TRYING TO REUNITE WITH FAITH

About a year later, Faith and I had dinner at Cognac on Lexington Avenue and 69th Street—the restaurant famously featured in *Sex and the City*, where Charlotte's water breaks and Mr. Big rushes her to the hospital.

It was a lovely evening. We were genuinely happy to see each other. Faith looked terrific—not a hair out of place—dressed in summer cashmere, stunning jewelry, and an elegant off-white outfit with matching low-heeled shoes. She loved René Mancini footwear, though I think these may have been Chanel.

Once the drinks and appetizers arrived, the conversation quickly shifted. Faith gently but persistently asked me to drop the legal matter between us. I responded, "But what about the money that's still owed to me?" She reassured me that everything would be resolved if I signed the release. It was an enjoyable dinner, but it was also a negotiation.

After her third drink, she confessed that the year before, she had only come home with five thousand dollars. I replied, *"Faith, why do you think I sued them? We couldn't live like this."* She nodded.

We even discussed the idea of her possibly leaving Douglas Elliman so we could work together again. I suggested we approach Robert Futterman at RKF. Faith asked, "Do you want me to reach out to Robert?"

Robert had become extremely successful since leaving Garrick-Aug about a decade before Faith and I did. But despite the warm tone of the evening, the trust between Faith and me had been damaged. I had the sense that the dinner was part of a broader attempt to settle the legal issue.

As someone who's negotiated professionally for nearly four decades, I've learned that negotiating with other brokers can be the most complicated of all. What should take a round or two can easily drag on for weeks.

In my heart, I didn't believe Faith would ever leave Douglas Elliman. And I hadn't forgotten that when I underwent a heart procedure, she hadn't reached out. I asked her that night, *"Why didn't you call me? I could have died."* She didn't answer.

When we parted ways that evening, we agreed to visit Jerry's grave together—but that never happened either.

The last legal case was still going through the New York Supreme Court, since the federal case had been dropped. Most of the case focused on how business expenses were handled over 10 years. That's when I learned about something in contract law called *"course of dealings."* It means that if two parties have followed the same pattern for a long time—even if some practices seem questionable—it can be seen as if both sides accepted it as part of their agreement. That made me stop and think. The process was draining. Faith continued to ask me to release her. My attorney grew less optimistic, perhaps sensing that our chances were limited. We explored settlement options, but the other side didn't move. Eventually, a counterclaim was filed against me. Douglas Elliman sued me stating that I owed them $500,000 dollars. As outrageous as it sounded, I understood in business litigation, anyone can sue—and then you must defend yourself. Knowing Howard Lorber was a certified public accountant, I knew Douglas Elliman could have created documents that I would have to prove false. In doing so, I would have to spend money and get an accountant to attest these were fabricated documents.

At that point, I realized I was operating in an arena that favored the other side. I decided it wasn't worth continuing. I chose to walk away. In doing so, I accepted that Douglas Elliman had more resources and leverage. I had already spent 14 intense and often difficult years with the firm. I didn't want to lose more time to something that could drag on for another decade.

Once I signed the release, a press announcement went out by Douglas Elliman stating that mutual terms had been reached. Yes, mutual terms were reached, I got my life back.

Forgiveness is something many people never learn in a lifetime. That night, I decided to forgive. Forgetting took longer—but I got there. I wished Faith well. I wished everyone involved in the matter peace and success. And I meant it.

XXXIII. THE INTERVIEWS

I started interviewing again and kept getting the same response—one that gave a whole new meaning to the word *"no."* People didn't know what had happened between Faith and me, and like any messy divorce, most preferred to keep their distance. No one wanted to take a side, so they simply took a pass.

One firm flat-out said, "You've got to be kidding." Another said, "I don't think so."

A gentleman from a top-tier firm; had agreed to meet. He brought me into a conference room and said, "Do you mind if I take a quick conference call?" He disappeared for 55 minutes. While I waited, I found the remote in the console and turned on the TV. When he finally returned, he looked at the screen and said, "You turned the TV on?" He wasn't amused. That interview wrapped up about ten minutes later.

At another large brokerage, I met with a very young woman in management. She wouldn't schedule a second interview without first producing my numbers. I explained that we had just moved apartments and I still had 25 boxes left to unpack in my living room — it would take some time. She just said, *"Call me then."*

It was clear she had no idea who I was. I tried leaning on my résumé and reputation and spurted out some of the transactions I was involved in, but it was wasted on her, I don't believe she read or was hearing what I said, for if she did, she would have asked around. She'd never heard of me, and truth be told, I'd never heard of her either — so I guess we were even.

Still, it was as if she didn't even know who Babe Ruth was. Babe was famous for two records: everyone knew he was the home-run king, but few realized he also held a record for strikeouts, either way, everyone knew the Babe. But she was young and she couldn't have cared less.

Then I sat down with the vice chairman of another major firm. I told him about running 11 health clubs, my 26-year run with Faith, and how I had built the Secret Brokers Society—an international network of commercial agents. I even pulled out four American passports, every page stamped from six of the seven continents that I did deals in or chased after some luxury tenant.

He looked at me and said, "Four passports? I've traveled a million miles on business."

"Yeah, but your company paid for it," I replied. "I did this on points and hustle. Can I get a little acknowledgement for that?"

I thanked him for his time and left.

At a certain point, I began to realize I might be intimidating these people. Not intentionally—it's just that when you walk into the room with decades of experience and a résumé that reads like a movie script, some folks get nervous. I was no longer in Kansas—and it was clear the Emerald City had new gatekeepers.

Still, I believed joining another firm—not starting from scratch—was the smarter move. So I persisted. But every interview followed the same pattern. I'd present my credentials, and then—like clockwork—the lawsuit would come up. And suddenly it was: "Thanks for coming by. We'll be in touch." They never were.

Eventually, I dropped down to the next tier—regional firms. I landed at Eastern Consolidated. Peter and Daun Hauspurg were absolute dolls. Married for over 30 years, they had built one of the city's most respected investment sales firms. They had a small retail group, and they gave me a desk. That was about it. I had lost 35 pounds, and Daun took notice. She referred to Faith's and my breakup as a "divorce."

I stayed for six weeks. Long enough to be grateful, short enough that most of the market didn't even know I was there. Shortly after I left, the company folded. A shock to everyone. They tried to sell but couldn't get their number. I think Peter and Daun saw the writing on the wall. The market had peaked, they weren't getting younger, and they wanted to travel.

We stayed in touch. I became Facebook friends with Daun and saw photos of them in the Sahara—on camels, dressed in desert garb. I was genuinely happy for them. Traveling with your mate is one of life's great joys.

Not long after, Peter passed away from a sudden heart attack. He was only in his mid-60s, the picture of health, and a class act. I'm grateful I got to know him—and Daun—better before he passed.

By Thanksgiving, I was in talks with a small Boston-based firm, who since changed names, merged or formed a new company. They had a small Manhattan satellite office — just four people. I met with the manager and two partners. One of them referred to me as "Grey Hairs," a backhanded way of saying I had experience.

That gig didn't last either.

A few months in, I had to fly to Northern Ireland to be with my father-in-law, who was dying. I stayed for a week. During that time, I called into the office several times — but the manager never took my calls. When I returned, he fired me. *"It's just not working out,"* he said.

Later, I found out why.

Joseph Benoit — a colleague from the Secret Brokers Society, an American expat living in Rome with his Italian wife and their beautiful twin daughters — had helped me get that job. When we spoke a month after I left, he asked, *"Why did you disappear for a week?"*

And that's when it clicked. The manager had lied to the owners. He never told them I was at my dying father-in-law's bedside.

I called the partners the next day to set the record straight. They apologized, but there was no path back — the office was too small.

I thanked them for the opportunity and moved on.

XXXIV: MENTAL HEALTH

U p to now, you've traveled with me all over the world — into places few ever go. You've stepped inside the Cartier mansion on Fifth Avenue, the Onassis offices in Athens and Mohamed Al-Fayed's private offices at Harrods in London. You were there when I met the CEO of Ferragamo in Florence, walked through Pierre Cardin's private garden, *Le Jardin de Cardin* and joined me shopping in the souk as I haggled with an Arab merchant who followed me endlessly, negotiating over a tin wine holder. Then that evening, at a local restaurant, belly dancers spun and twirled with candles balanced on their heads all in Marrakech. And you even entered the Room of Tears in Vatican City, just before Pope Benedict XVI resigned. We stayed in a bungalow at the Beverly Hills Hotel. where Hollywood's elite stayed. Faith and I helped clean up Times Square and sold a building to Carlos Slim—one that Elizabeth Taylor once lived in with her husband.

By this point in my journey, I was mentally and physically exhausted. If you're uncomfortable reading about mental health, I suggest you skip this chapter and the next.

One day, I sat down and wrote heartfelt letters to my wife, my sister, and to Faith. I wanted to express how much I loved them. Faith had hurt me badly and believed I had betrayed her. So many doors had closed and to many I was looked upon as a traitor. And yet, despite the pain I felt for Faith, I still missed her. After all, we had spent nearly every day together for 26 years—either in person, over the phone, or by text or email. As we can see by this book I can write, but this was the first time I had ever expressed myself in writing. I read the three letters aloud while visiting my sister and her fiancé.

Unfortunately, they misunderstood. They thought I was saying good-bye. My sister's fiancé gently but firmly urged me that I needed rest. He began explaining the services at a nearby hospital, suggesting that a weekend there—under professional care—might help me reset.

I had always associated places like that with luxury rehabs, the kind used by celebrities who were getting off a drug habit. But I was so emotionally drained, so desperate for peace and clarity, that I agreed. I got into the car and drove with him to the hospital, and I voluntarily signed myself in.

Unbeknownst to me, it was a State-run psychiatric facility.

I realized the gravity of the situation the moment they locked the door behind me. It was a very large clanging sound where they turned a huge lever and two bars crossed the door into the adjoining walls. I wasn't locked into a padded room, rather it was an entire floor of a psych ward with about sixty patients walking about freely.

Here's something most people don't know: you can sign yourself *in*, but you can't sign yourself *out*. I was now the property of the State subject to the discretion of two doctors who would decide when, or if, I was fit to leave.

I immediately felt trapped. I felt betrayed by my family. But in time, I believe they had the best of intentions—they just didn't understand the consequences. A week away on holiday may have been a simpler solution.

So let me tell you what it was like.

You are first stripped, legs spread open, and all your personal belongings are taken from you including your phone. Three times a day, I stood in line with the other patients to take medication—antidepressants that were also addictive. Having spent years in the health club industry, living clean, not even using a salt shaker since 1978, this was a shock to the system.

The staff—about six people—sat behind a three-foot partition at the ward entrance. The room that housed the medication was locked. When open, it looked like a small pharmacy. Meals were served in a communal dining hall. The other patients were mostly kind. The more manic individuals were kept under full observation, separate from the rest of us. Most of the patients were young and friendly. On nice days, we played basketball outdoors, ignoring the barbed wire that lined the top of the fence. There was a recreation room where we could shoot pool. Some patients had been through the system before.

My room had a single dresser and a platform bed with a foam mattress. There was no lock on the door. The bathroom had a shower stall, sink, and toilet. Everything was painted dark green or navy blue, with a single flickering fluorescent light overhead. I received fresh towels and sheets each day. But the entrance to the ward always stayed locked, so I could not leave.

A circular corridor wrapped around the ward, and patients walked it endlessly. Some held arms. It reminded me of the indoor tracks at the health clubs I used to manage—except here, everyone was medicated and most were expressionless.

There was one TV room where we all watched the same programs. I was allowed two visitors a day; mine usually came at night.

The problem was, I wanted to leave the next morning. But I was told, "No."

There was a sign on the wall outlining patient rights. According to my memory, it stated that the State had the right to keep you for up to 60 days under observation. That uncertainty—*not knowing* when I could leave—only increased my anxiety. I called my family. They couldn't do anything either. I think my sister began to realize a mistake had been made. My wife hadn't been part of the decision and was furious when she found out.

There were no therapy sessions. No one sat down with me to talk through what had happened or to help me heal. I was just observed—from a distance. The only time I saw a doctor was to determine whether I was fit to leave. And I had to wait—days—for them to return to the ward.

The good news? When I finally did meet with the lead doctors, they agreed to release me. I walked out of there on my birthday.

I left angry. I felt violated. I knew this experience would go on my record. But what could I do? I had hit rock bottom—and I had to move forward.

I hated the medications. They made my mind foggy. There's a massive pharmaceutical industry that profits from keeping people on these drugs. When you complain, they blame the prescription and simply change it for another one. Within two months, I went cold turkey. That was the end of it. Once I was off, my mind cleared—and I never went back.

The issue with that State-run ward was simple: there was no treatment, only sedation. No healing, just numbing. As mentioned, I made frequent calls from the one shared phone in the ward. It became my lifeline.

Still, I'm grateful for all of my life experiences — including this one. We are the sum of our stories, both large and small. Would I have preferred to skip this chapter? Of course. But it gave me the fire I needed to climb back up the mountain — and that's why I wanted to share it with you, the reader. Because that's exactly what I did.

I could have chosen not to write this story, too. But maybe someone out there can benefit from my experience.

XXXV. FINDING MYSELF

Since I had walked away from the lawsuit, we sold the apartment at the height of the market, in December 2017. We got a good price and decided to rent our next one.

It was Christmas, and we had just moved into a building in the high 70s on First Avenue. At the time, I was deeply low-spirited. Everything I had worked for had been taken away—my colleagues in the business had rejected me and looked down on me, I was still feeling the loss of my partnership with Faith and was reeling from the betrayal. I was still feeling the effects of the medication, not yet going cold-turkey. Douglas Elliman did what they felt they had to do when they threw me out—in spite of their behavior, they wanted to protect their brand. But the way they treated me was appalling, something no one should have to endure. Faith and I were good people, and yet they exploited us completely—and then, to make matters worse, they tore us apart.

I felt like Dalton Trumbo, the screenwriter who was blackballed by the film industry for his politics. I couldn't see a future for myself. Twice, I went down into the subway, sat on a public bench, and watched train after train go by, trying to summon the courage to end it all.

The previous year, I had been falsely and mistakenly committed to a mental institution after writing three heartfelt letters to my family — letters meant simply as expressions of love and gratitude, which they tragically misinterpreted as suicide notes. I never said I was going to take my own life.

But now, with that unfair mark on my otherwise spotless record, and feeling trapped at a dead end in my career with no future in sight, I found myself actually thinking about it for the first time. There was no question now — I had finally "hit rock bottom."

To my blessings, the first time I sat on a public bench on that platform, a saxophone player was there, playing some of my favorite tunes. Somehow, hearing him convinced me to go upstairs and walk back to my apartment. The second time – one week later, I returned to the subway watching the trains rush by again. A guitarist was there, playing and singing Beatles songs. I had grown up on the Beatles—I first saw them on *The Ed Sullivan Show*, and I shared a birthday with John Lennon, October 9th. I adored them as a boy and followed them throughout their careers.

My guardian angel was surely with me on those two days, sending just the right musicians and just the right songs to remind me that life is still good. I knew of a few suicides in the real estate industry. The business is built on "feast or famine—you eat what you kill." I've always hated that expression. But my situation felt even darker than just having a few bad years in sales; I felt as though the entire industry was against me, not knowing the true story.

Now that the subject has come up, I believe the industry should establish a suicide prevention program, because I know my experience is not unique. Many others have faced the same darkness, and no one should have to face it alone. Professionals could step in to help struggling salespeople reboot their careers — offering leads, guidance, and emotional support.

As bleak as things seemed, I couldn't bring myself to go through with it. I went back home. More than anything, I loved my wife too much. I knew that if I ended my life, it would have devastated her — and I couldn't do that to her.

Right after this I reconnected with Lisa Keys, one of Faith's and my former assistants, and I told her what had happened to me by phone. She said, "Yes, I read some of the press you got." We agreed to meet and she came to the lobby of my building to say hi. Once we had chatted and spent some time together and I had told her my story, she said, "You're strong and you're going to be fine." Having known Lisa for more than 10 years, I felt what she said was true and I knew it was just going to take some time to get over what I had gone through.

Since those dark days, I've taken up tennis regularly — and I'm still quite the competitor. I approach the game the same way I approach brokerage: fast and hard. Over time, I came to understand why I stayed in brokerage as long as I did. Like tennis, it teaches you how to recover when you miss a shot or lose a point — to keep moving forward and never look back. You can't afford to be your own worst enemy or waste time beating yourself up. You have to learn how to love yourself — and keep loving yourself, no matter what. Because here's another truth: if you don't love yourself, it's hard to truly love someone else.

During my return journey, as Frank Sinatra once sang, "*I just pick myself up and get back in the race*" I started listening to Joel Osteen, the evangelist, on You-Tube and he was inspirational. Years back it was motivational speaker Tony Robbins who had helped me get focused, but now it was Joel Osteen and I loved his messages. I would listen to as many as five of his testimonials on some days. I have always believed in God and have always had a strong connection with my faith. I knew things happened for a reason and better days were on the way. I only had to be patient and continue to work. I knew things would eventually come together.

Five months into the new apartment, I said, *"I'm not happy here. We've got to find something better."* Many stores in the area were closed, and a new development project was underway across the street. The area was depressing looking. I also felt out of the mainstream—we were living too far north, and my wife had a long walk to the subway station.

"But we have seven months left on our lease," my wife said. *"How are you going to handle that?"*

"Don't worry. I'm a real estate broker."

She just gave me one of those looks only a wife can give her husband.

We found a larger apartment just a few blocks from Central Park — twice the size of our Upper East Side place, with twelve windows, a wood-burning fireplace, and two entrances — all for just $500 more a month. A steal. Before we moved out, I hired a broker and arranged for her to sublease our old apartment. But on moving day, as I handed the keys to the doorman on our way out, he stopped me and said, *"Mr. Aquino, I can't accept these keys. You need to see management on the fourth floor."*

I felt apprehensive, like I was being called to the dean's office. But the building manager smiled and said, *"Mr. Aquino, we're sorry to see you go. We saw in one of your emails that you know the president of our firm."*

"Only for about 30 years," I replied.

The manager smiled wider. *"Great. If you give us the keys, we'll rent the apartment for you."*

I couldn't believe what she was saying. I asked her to repeat it, since I still owed the property owner seven months' rent. She did—and I happily handed over the keys. Within two weeks, they had rented the apartment and returned my security deposit.

Things were certainly looking up. My belief in God was stronger than ever.

XXXVI. TRAGIC NEWS AND THE TRUTH

Several years after my leaving Douglas Elliman, two days before Christmas, I was having breakfast at a diner near my apartment and I got a call from Linda Alexander, who had represented Faith and me for years. She told me that Faith had passed away the previous day. I immediately broke down and cried like a baby. The owner and the waitresses came over, asking if I was okay. I said, "I just found out my best friend passed away." They brought me water. I said to Linda, "What happened?" She explained that Faith had been found on the floor of her Fifth Avenue apartment in her dressing gown. She had died of a heart attack. I thought that was especially sad, since she used to spend Christmas Eve with my family and me.

Several days prior to Faith's death my voice teacher, who is a practicing Christian, gave me a gift for Christmas. It was a huge box, beautifully wrapped. When my wife came to my office, she insisted that I open it there and then. I wanted to wait for Christmas Eve, which was several days away. She said, "No, let's open it now." How can you refuse the wife regarding Christmas? The box was on the other side of my desk on the floor and my desk had a small two foot partition on top of the desk that I would post To-do notes. I could not see the box. My wife bent over and for a moment, I could not see my wife either. Suddenly, she jumped like a cat on a hot tin roof. I said, "What happened?" She - in shock.

She showed me all the items in the box. They were all inscribed with the word "Faith." There were mugs that said "Faith," a flash drive that said "Faith," a leather-bound book that said *Faith - That Overcomes,* and a Christian CD by Joyce Meyer, called *"Growing In Faith."* My voice teacher wouldn't have known how all of these impacted me.

On the next day, Faith passed away and I heard the news the following morning. I saw this gift as a sign of Faith's leaving and saying goodbye to me.

The memorial service was by invitation only, and all the press were invited. I wasn't.

Faith was hailed as the Queen of Retail.

Faith died on a Friday and I learned she was cremated on Monday. To do this, clearance has to be received from the City Coroner. The only problem was that between Friday and Monday there was Christmas, so I am not sure how it was done so quickly.

Five days after Faith's death, Dotty Herman announced she was selling her shares back to Howard Lorber's company for an amount I thought was close to what she had bought the company for 15 years earlier. That is still a mystery: why she sold one week after Faith's death, what a coincidence. Howard lost two power-house women within a week.

When Dotty had bought Insignia Douglas Elliman, along with Howard and Prudential, the *New York Post* reported that they paid $73.5 million. If you divide that number into three, the amount comes to about $24.5 million each. Now, Dotty agreed to sell her shares of the company, about fifteen years later back to one of Howard's companies for $40 million. The company was about three times the size they bought it. What interested me about this sale was that she agreed to a payment plan. The trades said she would get $10 million dollars on the closing in early 2019 and then get quarterly amounts from January 1, 2020, ending October 2022.

I wonder if that payment plan was honored, since it ran through the height of the Covid pandemic.

Now, Howard would be running the company on his own. Dotty would still be CEO, but what is that old expression about the golden rule? Whoever holds the gold, rules!

Immediately upon Faith's death, the *New York Times* ran the following headline: "Faith Hope Consolo, a Force in Retail Real Estate, Is Dead at 73"

The *New York Post*: "Faith Hope Consolo, New York Real Estate Legend, dead at 73"

Women's Wear Daily: "Queen of Retail dies at 69"

Other publications referred to Faith as,"The Retail Mega Broker," and "The Legend."

All these articles can be found on-line and on my website, memoirsofawatchsalesman.com/photos.

I revealed on LinkedIn how my old partner and best friend had passed with a beautiful photo of her. Within a couple of days, I received more than 400,000 postings. For a second blog post on LinkedIn, I received another 250,000 postings with people's sympathy gestures.

The following week, I went to visit the cemetery where her former mate Jerry was buried, thinking I would see a freshly open gravesite, but it wasn't there.

All the stories honored her legacy and they went into detail as to where she was from and who her parents had been. They wrote that she was born in the affluent town of Shaker Heights, Ohio, and then moved to Westport, Conn. when she was two years old, after her father had died who was a developer. She attended Miss Porter's school. Shortly thereafter, a childhood friend of Faith's sent the *New York Times* reporter who had written the obituary a note via LinkedIn and told her the

Faith story had all been made up. She said it straight, with all the facts. The same *Times* reporter then released a follow-up:

She Fooled An Entire Industry With Her Lies

by Julie Satow

Ms. Satow went on to tell the real story, going into considerable detail about Faith's life. Faith was from a working-class neighborhood in Cleveland. Her dad did not die when she was two; rather, he had lived into his 90s. He had been incarcerated in a federal prison for selling kilos of heroin. His case was the first time the word "kilos," along with the word "heroin," was used in an Ohio newspaper.

Faith's mom was not a child psychiatrist, and she did not write books with the child psychiatrist Gesell. She was a hairdresser who worked in Martin's department store, in Brooklyn, where my sister had worked in the cosmetics department. Her mom was not English; rather, her roots were in Ireland, like my wife who is from Belfast.

Lastly, Faith had lived 10 blocks from me in Brooklyn when I was a boy. We had been confirmed at the same church: St. Brendan's on Avenue O and East 12th Street. Faith had attended St. Brendan's all-girls school while I went to P.S. 199, down the block. Both schools were located on East 12th Street. Hers was on Avenue O and mine was between Avenue M and N. She lived nearby, at Avenue T and 11th Street (which was called Coney Island Avenue), and I lived on Avenue L and East 16th Street. Faith for me, was almost literally the girl next door, but remember, she was ten years my senior, so it was unlikely I would have known her through school or church.

Her father's name had been Frank, not John. In his obituary, it said he was an honored disabled World War II veteran and after the war, he was an administrator to the Free Youth Foundation Program, a program for juvenile delinquents. During WWII, if you were willing to fight on the frontlines, as long as you didn't murder anyone, you were sent to fight for your country.

After Frank and Faith's mother divorced, and after he served in the war, Frank was married to Bonnie, who had no arms. When Frank came back to the States, he met and married her and had a family. He made a famous documentary movie on her life, which he produced, for which he received an Academy Award nomination. It is called *The Life of Bonnie Consolo*. You can find it on You Tube, it's amazing.

Ever since I was introduced to Frank via that *Times* article, and then his obituary, I believed that he was a kind man with a huge heart , who loved his family, who simply went down the wrong path. You can see Frank on the video documentary sitting at the kitchen table as Bonnie is cooking. Bonnie was another amazing person. She cooked and served dinner with both her feet while on a high stool chair with wheels on the bottom. You can see her at the kitchen sink, washing and cutting vegetables both with her feet. She pushed herself with ease from one side of the kitchen to the next, like the Olympian ice skater Peggy Fleming on a bar stool with wheels. She drove, shopped, and did everything that everyone else did, just with her feet. She was fabulous.

I recall another situation from which I might have realized Faith's story was make-believe. One time, we were at a diner in Westport, Connecticut. She had made up a story as to how she had worked there as a teen. I was hoping she would take me to see her grandmother's house, which I had heard about for more than 25 years. She went quiet and I thought she got melancholy, so I did not push the subject further. As we know now, grandmother's house was located at Homecrest Court, a half block from Avenue T in Brooklyn—not in Westport.

Lastly, when her staff cleaned out her desk after her death, they found a license that said, "Faith Goldstein." I found out from a good friend of hers who happened to live on a block near Prospect Park, where I lived as a child, that Faith had been married to a Marty Goldstein and they had lived on Ocean Parkway in Brooklyn.

I was told he had been violently abusive to Faith. Faith spun that story too, telling me she had been married and had moved to Santa Monica, Calif., where she and her husband had a health club business that catered to the rich and famous. Maybe she spun that story because she knew I had been in that business. She said she parked the members' cars by their color. We would laugh every time she told that story.

Faith told me that one day he had driven their Rolls Royce into their swimming pool. That's when she decided to leave, and flew back to New York City with only the fur coat on her back.

I believe the abuse happened, but I think it was in Brooklyn. Faith also mentioned, several times in our relationship, that her mom had been best friends with Bishop Fulton Sheen, and that he recorded his famous TV series in her mom's library in Westport. When the Sheen Center for Thought and Culture opened, at 18 Bleecker Street in Manhattan, I wanted to take Faith there, not realizing that she had made up this story too.

It took a few years to learn what they did with Faith's ashes. Finally, her friend, Esther Mueller, who runs the eponymous real estate school, Esther Mueller Academy, said that her friends sprinkled her ashes over Jerry's grave. He was buried in a Jewish cemetery and anyone who knows Jewish law will tell you that only a Jewish person can be buried there.

So here I am, on my own again. Going solo is a feeling I know all too well. I've always liked partnerships, but here's how it played out: I went from a real estate company with Faith and 50 people, which eventually dwindled down to just the two of us — Faith and me. And now, Faith is long gone, and I'm on my own.

I have to say, those sixteen years working side by side with Faith, without the backing of Garrick-Aug Store Leasing, made me a stronger broker. We had to figure it out ourselves, and we did. With technology, the power of CoStar and their database with all the commercial listings at our fingertips, plus great admin and marketing support that Faith surrounded herself with, we didn't just survive — we thrived. In fact, we continued to be leaders in the industry.

Looking back, it's clear to me that going out on my own two years before Faith's death may have been the best decision I ever made. If I had stayed by her side until the very end, I would have been devastated.

After her passing in July 2019, Douglas Elliman announced the formation of "The Faith Consolo Team." That amazed me — this was the team I had helped build and nurture over 26 years. But I stood back and simply watched.

The team consisted of Arthur Maglio, who had handled Harlem for us, and two newcomers: Corey Shuster and Diana Zisholtz. Corey had just finished school in London, and Diana had once been Faith's summer intern — my wife and I had even attended her wedding before she joined Faith.

A year later, Arthur told me that Douglas Elliman / Howard Lorber wanted a fee for them to continue to use The Faith Team name. The team politely said, "No." And that's that story.

XXXVII. AFTER FAITH'S DEATH

A friend, Joanna Capobianco, told me that Faith had suffered a major heart attack about a week prior and had been hospitalized. She had checked herself out against medical advice, and the doctor reportedly said, "Faith, do you know how sick you are?" I believe she knew her days were numbered and chose to pass in the privacy of her Fifth Avenue apartment.

Another friend told me that Faith had called Viand, her regular coffee shop on Madison Avenue, to have her usual oatmeal and coffee delivered. When the delivery person arrived and got no response at her door, the doorman sent someone upstairs to check on her. They found Faith lying on the floor, wearing her cream-colored silk charmeuse robe and matching silk slippers, each adorned with a fur trim and a rhinestone at the center. The coroner later confirmed she had died of a heart attack caused by arteriosclerosis.

In the days following her death, people called me—some to share warm memories, others to vent. Faith had her admirers and her critics. Some people just couldn't stand her. She was beautiful, intelligent, assertive, well-respected, worldly, and always in the media. She had many loyal clients and customers. William Rudin, President of Rudin Management, summed it up best in the *New York Times* obituary:

> "She really changed the retail marketplace. Her street smarts, entrepreneurial spirit, and flair—even the way she

dressed and communicated—attracted an amazing clientele, some of the great international brands to New York."

Even when I encountered people in person, I could tell many assumed I was one of the "Faith haters," not knowing the real story—how *The Real Deal* published a false narrative pushed by Douglas Elliman without fact-checking.

After we parted ways professionally, Faith gained a significant amount of weight. I had always helped manage her health and encouraged regular doctor visits. We used to sit in waiting rooms together like two kids. But after we split, she put on at least 40 pounds. In one photo, she looked very heavy—though her face remained beautiful, with flawless skin and hardly a wrinkle.

She also began drinking heavily, according to one of her former assistants. She was said to be taking several medications with serious side effects. A young woman once told me she had met Faith at a REBNY black tie cocktail party prior to the annual dinner and that Faith could barely walk. She asked her if she didn't mind if she would go to the bar and get her a glass of champagne complaining that her shoes were too tight.

After our split, Karen Dome grew closer to Faith. She told a friend that she was the one who held Faith together and made sure she had someplace to go during the holidays. But Karen never knew the full story — only what she'd read in the press. JoAnna told me that Faith would often vent her anger about me, saying I had "destroyed everything." JoAnna would gently push back, telling her, *"That's not Joey."*

After Faith's death, more of her story quietly came to light — that she had grown up in a working-class family in Brooklyn. While many wear their humble beginnings as a badge of honor, Faith tried to rewrite her past. As an old friend, I understood why. One likely reason was that she didn't want the industry to know her father had spent time in federal prison. In that context, her silence made sense to me — and I complete-ly understood her choice.

XXXVIII. MY PRESS AND WRITINGS

Back then, if you Googled my name, a parade of headlines would pop up about how I had sued Faith and Douglas Elliman. That episode became like a permanent tattoo on my name — loud, visible, and hard to erase. The stories, mostly exaggerated and fueled by lazy or perhaps even malicious reporting, were splashed across *The Real Deal* and other outlets. I realized the only way to push them down the search rankings was to fight back the only way I knew how: with my own press, my own words, and my own truth. If search engines favored the most recent stories, then I would bury the old ones with better ones.

The only honest reporting came from *The New York Real Estate Journal*, by my friend Kristine Wolf, and *Real Estate Weekly*, by another good friend, Linda Barr.

So I picked up the phone and called Amir Korangy, publisher and co-founder of *The Real Deal*, to see if he'd finally take the stories down. I told him the reporting was incorrect. Faith didn't spend $1 million of my commissions —"Sorry, Joe," he said, "they're not coming down." End of call.

Fine. If they wouldn't rewrite the record, I'd write my own.

Jeff Mann at *The Mann Report* gave me a monthly column, and I started by writing about the global cities I'd visited. I shared some great pieces with him — one about Belfast, Northern Ireland, which had grown from hosting just two cruise ships a year to over 150, and how the Titanic Museum was attracting more visitors than the Eiffel Tower in Paris. I also wrote about the fabulous luxury shopping in São Paulo, Brazil, where the staff insists you sit down for an espresso, offers the use of their luxurious bathrooms, and treats you with the warmest hospitality.

After the second article, Jeff called me and said, *"Joe, we're a local paper — stick to New York."* I thanked him, as I wasn't in a New York state of mind, as I was already planning my next trip — to Venice.

Real Estate Weekly was more open. Linda Barr, the editor, had been fair with her coverage during the lawsuit, and she welcomed my submissions. Kristine Wolf from the *New York Real Estate Journal* went a step further—she offered me a regular 750-word column. I took the challenge. Kristine's paper had also been one of the few along with Real Estate Weekly that gave honest reporting when I needed it most.

Back when Faith and I were a team, we had two publicists who handled all the writing. I edited quietly behind the scenes, but the bylines always went to Faith. My name appeared only if we closed a deal together — and even then, I was usually in the background. Unless someone decided to profile me — which happened maybe once every five or six years — I was invisible.

But after our split, it was finally my time to write. At first, it felt foreign. But soon I found my rhythm. After all those years of doing deals in Manhattan and across the country — and traveling the world for business — I had plenty to say. The articles started getting published. I knew I hadn't quite mastered the Queen's English — but let's be honest, how many Brooklyn guys do? To sharpen my prose without watering it down, I reached out to a former *Wall Street Journal* reporter who'd moved to the Midwest. He helped me refine the writing while keeping my voice intact. I was more concerned about using correct grammar, since I never had any trouble telling a story or making a point.

As I had done for years building Faith Hope Consolo's brand, I now turned that same energy to promoting my own firm. I rebranded it as JAACRES—short for *Joseph A. Aquino Commercial Real Estate Services*—and pronounced *Jay-Cres*. I didn't do it to be clever. I did it because when people searched my name, they landed on garbage. The rebrand was my way of starting fresh while still honoring the name I built. They began showing up on Google. Search "Joseph Aquino" or "JAACRES," and you'll see a plethora of pieces I've written.

Despite all the roadblocks that followed me from the day I filed that first lawsuit in May 2015, five years later, I still had fire in my belly. I still loved the business. And frankly, I had no choice. I played the cards I was dealt—and I played them hard

XXXIX. VENICE AND THE NEW OFFICE

I was in Venice at the FT Luxury Summit. I had just met the head designer of Balenciaga, Denna Gvasalia. He had crossed the room during a break to give me a nice compliment on my double-breasted grey glen plaid suit, with its six-inch lapels. I must admit, this suit made me feel and look like Marcelo Mastroianni, some other may say John Gotti. ...that's a joke, I whispered to Gvasalia that I had bought this suit on sale for $500 on a close-out on Madison Avenue and he said, "I don't care what the cost was, that's a great suit." We both laughed and I said to myself, "If next year he comes out with wider lapels, I'll know where he got the inspiration from."

Then I saw Linda Alexander's husband, Tar Beaty, a well-known commercial artist whom I knew personally and from Facebook. He had been posting photos of Venice. I messaged him, "Tar, are you in Venice?"

He said, "Yes, I'm here, why?,

"I replied, I'm here too, this is my last day. I'm at The FT Luxury conference. Please send my love to Linda and tell her I am taking her out to lunch in a few weeks."

Two weeks later, Linda and I were having lunch at Fred's restaurant on the ninth floor of Barney's, on Madison Avenue. It's closed now, but it was an incredible meeting place with wrap-around windows that gave a view of the neighborhood's rooftops. It was a place to see and be seen. That day, Vera Wang was sitting at the next table.

It was good to see Linda. We talked a lot. We discussed Faith's death and how she had stopped working with Linda, too. I knew that once I left Faith, she couldn't afford to keep up all those expenses. I tried explaining that to Linda, but she was still upset with Faith and didn't accept the explanation.

Finally, after a lovely lunch and catching up with Linda, I went in for the close and said, "I am looking for an office. Do you have one for me at your place?"

"Debra Hazel's office just became available. She just left for a WeWorks space near her home." Linda and I quickly came to a rental number. With the passing of Faith, I needed to be with a friend, so it was a big help to go to Linda's office daily and see a friendly face with someone who was inspired to see me do well.

I immediately hired Bela Gospodinova, of Brand + Refine, who had been one of Faith and my assistants. Now she had her own company and she put together one of the best branding programs, for me, that I had seen in years. With the new office and branding, business was on the upswing.

XL: DONER KEBAB; LONDON; THE AMERICAN DREAM

I've always loved Apple products—but for some reason, the iPhone X didn't love me back. It kept glitching, so I found myself becoming a regular at the Apple flagship on Fifth Avenue, right across from the Plaza Hotel. Doesn't matter what time of day or night you go—Apple's always packed. Even on a quiet Sunday evening, I had to book an appointment and wait an hour to see a technician.

So I walked across the street and slipped into the Palm Court at the Plaza for a glass of champagne. It was peaceful. Elegant. Then a lively group of men sat down at the bar, about ten feet away. They looked like a jolly crew, so I struck up a conversation — something I've never been shy about. They even ended up buying me a drink.

Turns out they were execs from a fast-growing fast-food company called German Doner Kebab (GDK). They already had 70 locations across the U.K. and Northern Europe and were now eyeing New York. I mentioned I'd be in London the following week, and one of them offered to set up a meeting with their GM so I could visit a store in person.

A week later, I was standing in one of their London locations. Bright orange interiors, a long line of customers, meat slowly rotating on vertical spits. The place was spotless and humming. I met the GM, who gave me a tour of the kitchen—compact but efficient. Not an inch of space was wasted. Then came my first kebab. It was delicious. I finally understood why Brits crave them after a night at the pub.

As I stood there, watching the steady stream of customers, my mind was already racing: *Where do I put this in New York?*

Back in Manhattan, I met the franchise head and the U.S. CEO for coffee in Bryant Park. I gave them the full pitch. I told them I had rolled out 40 Au Bon Pain locations across the city and would deliver a study of 30 site options in a week. They looked at me like I was crazy. I shrugged and said, "That's what I do." I told them how I started as a street canvasser and knew every block of New York like the back of my hand.

And I delivered. In under a week, I handed them a shortlist of prime locations: Harlem's hottest corner, the Garment Center, Times Square, Midtown East, Chelsea, Gramercy Park, Soho. We toured together, and I got a sense of their preferences. A few days later, I took their top decision-maker on another round. We worked at it for six months, trying to make a deal happen. But for one reason or another, nothing stuck.

Then I went to an entertainment convention in Los Angeles and met Corey Lober from the American Dream Mall in East Rutherford, New Jersey. She told me about the massive project her company had taken over—originally called Xanadu. I remembered the name, but had never visited.

She described a mall that was 70% entertainment and 30% retail—complete with a DreamWorks waterpark, a Nickelodeon Universe ride park, the first indoor ski slope in the Northeast, and an NHL-sized ice rink. "Come see it next week," she said.

When I arrived, they handed me work boots, a hard hat, and an iridescent vest, then whisked me away on a golf cart. It was like a tour of the future. I'd never seen anything like it. As soon as I got back to the office, I started calling clients and setting up tours.

I brought in German Doner Kebab. They got it immediately. The franchisee picked a 2,600-square-foot space on the second level—overlooking the skating rink, steps from the waterpark and kids' rides. Prime visibility.

Over the next few years, I traveled back to London several times and formed a partnership with Lunson Mitchenall, a powerhouse retail firm. I also built a relationship in Austin, Texas, with The Weitzman Group—leaders in their market. Both partnerships expanded my national and international reach. Later on I brought in James Andrew International from London that assisted me with the brokerage sale of Hotels.

That same year, I did nine deals out of Linda's office—four of them with Charleston Shoes. Lynne Anne San Andres from Mason Alexander brought the brand to me, and together we moved fast—like Johnny Rockets fast. We secured locations on Jobs Lane in Southampton, Sixth Avenue in the Plaza District, Soho, and Newbury Street in Boston—all within 60 days. That's unheard of doing that many in such a short time period.

I also worked with Sherle Wagner, the luxury bathroom fixture brand that's been around for nearly a century. I sold their Los Angeles showroom in the Design District, then found them a full-floor showroom on Madison Avenue—above Jimmy Choo, right next to Hermès. That assignment took just six months, lightning speed for a deal of that caliber. Leading the charge in the sale of Sherle Wagner's Los Angeles retail / showroom was Anthony Palermo. He represented the buyer and I represented the seller. Vince Geoffrey – Sherle Wagner's owner – got close to $6 million for the sale. I later worked with his son Evan for the NYC showroom. Anthony is one of the premier brokers in Los Angeles. Over the years together we did four deals in total. Besides Sherle

Wagner, we leased LOL Kids a store along Sunset Boulevard, MonnaLisa childrenswear along N. Beverly Drive, both in Beverly Hills, Los Angeles and Perrin Paris 1893 along Madison Avenue in Manhattan,. Anthony brought me the tenant and I found the space.

Looking back on that year, I was amazed — deals in Manhattan, Southampton, Boston, Beverly Hills, partnerships in London and Austin, and the relaunch of the Secret Brokers Society. Not bad for a guy just waiting for his Genius Bar appointment, who just got back from Venice.

XLI. SUMMING UP

Now I resumed my monthly calls with the Secret Brokers Society team that I had put together 14 years before. I did a mailing celebrating this milestone, stating, " The Secret Broker Society is now officially a teenager." It has a combination of 30 international and national brokers. When the pandemic hit, this networking effort was especially important since the calls were somewhat cathartic. Everyone shared information on how Covid was spreading in the United States. We were also hearing about the effects of Covid on other countries.

During the pandemic, I helped a lot of people with their leases. Retail sales had stopped, yet tenants were still expected to pay rent. It was a tough time for everyone. Months into the pandemic, some of my customers had to relocate, and I was able to assist them.

I helped Mandelli from Milano secure a new office lease at 5 East 57th Street, across from Tiffany & Co. Amas, a 50-year-old music and entertainment group, moved into rehearsal and office space at the Film Center Building on the edge of Times Square.

As we got further from the heart of COVID and things began returning to some normalcy, I found a prime retail location for Organic by John Patrick in Bridgehampton, right next to my favorite French restaurant, Pierre's. I assisted Paul Morelli Jewelers with their new Madison Avenue location, positioning them diagonally across from the new Hermès flagship.

In addition, I completed two more Madison Avenue deals: Mademoiselle Mirabelle boutique and Collette Home from Southampton. Then, Olivia Balsamo of OAB Realty and I helped a furniture tenant secure a 70,000-square-foot showroom in Long Island City, Queens.

And during it all, I also wrote these memoirs.

On my watch, I've seen entire neighborhoods transform—some revitalized, others reimagined and renamed. From the resurgence of SoHo, Times Square, and the Meatpacking District to the creation of new identities like NoLIta, NoHo, DUMBO, Hudson Yards, Bleecker Street and Alphabet City, I've witnessed New York constantly reinvent itself. I've also watched countless entrepreneurs rise again—rebuilding not just businesses, but entire real estate sectors—like Ian Schrager, who was one of the founders of Studio 54. He went to prison for tax evasion, but on his release went from night club king, to a hotel maven who branded properties like the Morgan, the Royalton and the Paramount—and then created the Public Hotel on the Lower East Side and partnered with Marriott on the trendy boutique Edition Hotels. All cool hotels.

I've seen a major New York property owner become President of the United States. I was here in New York City on the day terrorists flew two planes into the World Trade Center. I know Larry Silverstein, who started as a real estate broker, became a property owner and then a developer, and watched his property — the World Trade Center — destroyed, only to rebuild the complex and name one of the buildings Freedom Tower.

I've seen a 100-plus-year-old Broadway theatre moved down the street on railroad tracks and totally restored. I've seen other old turn of the century theatres developed by entertainment companies and corporate sponsors. I started in business when we used typewriters with carbon paper, white out and index cards for your customers' contact information. (If you were really organized, you used a Rolodex, which compiled all these cards in one big cylinder that turned in alphabetical order.) I come from a time where we didn't do an email blast to thousands of people or have 6,000 friends on Facebook and LinkedIn. Instead, we called people on the telephone that had a wire attached to it. We called the process "dialing for dollars" because we didn't have push-button phones yet, they were rotary dials.

I've seen an entire neighborhood built over 28 acres of train tracks — something no one ever imagined possible. What an engineering feat that was.

Now, slowly but surely, we're seeing New York City's piers and docks come back to life after more than 50 years of dormancy, with venues like City Winery and their fabulous music space on 11th Avenue and 15th Street at Pier 57. They have a great restaurant and bar, and you can catch some of the best live musical acts. Their lineup is always star-studded.

They feature both new and established artists. One of the best Beatles cover bands, Strawberry Fields, regularly performs full Beatles albums from start to finish — I've seen them play *Abbey Road* and *Rubber Soul* note for note. I also saw the original Yardbirds perform *I'm a Man* and *Heart Full of Soul*, and they were fantastic.

I'm actually helping City Winery find a location in London; they'll do great there. They need at least 20,000 going up to 30,000 square feet. On top of everything, they also produce their own wine, which is exceptionally good.

My dad was a longshoreman, and I still remember when all the piers and docks were alive with commercial activity. Now, City Winery has brought that energy back — knocking it out of the park every night and on weekends. Another spot my wife and I frequent is Brookfield Place in Battery Park, right on the Hudson River in FiDi — short for the Financial District. It's one of the hottest destinations in the city, with luxury retailers like Gucci and some of the finest restaurants, all offering breathtaking views of Jersey City, Ellis Island, and our iconic Statue of Liberty.

Now, as we wait for driverless cars and more artificial intelligence to dominate our lives, we must be careful not to lose our souls. We must not let technology take over the decision-making in our lives. The *"takeaway"* I hope one gets from this book is that I had fun navigating through life, having made some great friendships and relationships along the way—and personally growing with the challenges. If I can give you only one piece of advice, it's this: "The easy road is not often the best road taken." The easy road doesn't give you the experience that you need to get to the next challenge.

We all have regrets. Sometimes I wonder how far I might have gone if I'd earned an MBA. Sure, it would have made me more corporate — But then again, I was already corporate. At its peak in the 1980s, Bally Fitness was generating over a billion dollars a year, and I brought my health club to the number two position in profitability in the Greater New York region — the company's largest market — a spectacular feat. Those numbers and accomplishments are impressive even today — and especially back then, in a young, fast-growing industry.

As I mentioned earlier, I was fortunate enough to attend Aviation High School in Long Island City, Queens. The Federal Aviation Administration oversaw all of our shop programs, preparing us for two mechanical licenses to work on airplanes — one for the power plant, and the other for the airframe. That school taught me to think big and solve problems on my own two feet. So in the end, I did just fine without an advanced degree.

These days, I sleep well and wake up happy every morning, immediately turning on the music at a high volume — though my wife hates it, so I lower the sound. And as I shared earlier, I've learned to forgive... though forgetting takes a little longer. Grudges don't serve your present — but they can fuel your drive and I love to play tennis. I do about twenty different stretches before the start of the day I play tennis, covering every body part. That's another great take – away from running health clubs, you know how to take care of your most important machine, your body.

When the news broke that Lorber was implicated in the civil case, I texted the article to Dotty Herman — his former partner, the one who had originally brought him into residential real estate back when he was still selling cigarettes and hot dogs. Her reply was simple: *"He destroyed the company."* I agreed.

A moment later, after I replied, she added: *"He gave me a nervous breakdown."*

I could empathize with Dotty, because Lorber had nearly broken me too — taking my money, driving a wedge between me and Faith, and tarnishing my reputation in the industry with a false, sensationalized narrative. I truly believe Faith might still be alive if she hadn't been drawn into such toxic company.

"Life is what happens to you while you're busy making other plans." John Lennon made that line famous, but it was originally written by Allen Saunders in *Reader's Digest* in 1957. That quote says it all: enjoy the ride, as much as the results.

My wife once told me that if I go before her, she'll have *"La Dolce Vita"* carved on my tombstone. *The Sweet Life.* And she's right — life is sweet. But you have to make it so, wherever you are.

And so, in closing — remember this:

No matter how hard you get knocked down...

come up swinging.

ABOUT THE AUTHOR

Joseph A. Aquino is the President of JAACRES, a commercial real estate brokerage firm based in Manhattan. He resides there with his wife Suzanne.

There are three things that will endure
FAITH, HOPE, and LOVE
and the greatest of these is
LOVE
— 1 Corinthians 13:13

Photos, letters, and articles can be found at:
www.memoirsofawatchsalesman.com/photos

Some of the Tenants We've Worked With Over the Years

Australia
Crumpler, Jan Logan, Oroton

Belgium
Godiva

Canada
Bitton / Buffalo Jeans, Holt Renfrew, Kookai, Le Chateau, Ports 1961

France
Arche, Berluti, Breuer, Cartier, Céline, Chloé, Daum, Diabless, Emanuel Ungaro, Fauchon Paris, Fresh, Hermès, Jacadi, Jean Paul Gaultier, Kusmi Tea Paris, Lacoste, Lalique, Longchamp Paris, Nina Ricci, Roche Bobois, Thierry Rabotin, Yves Saint Laurent, Walter Steiger

Germany
Bogner, Etienne Aigner, Hugo Boss, Jil Sander, Joop!, Lumas, MCM, Mondi, Montblanc, Porsche, Rena Lange, Wempe

Great Britain
Anya Hindmarch, Aquascutum, Creed, Daks, Gina, Jimmy Choo, Molton Brown, Myla, Ozwald Boateng, Paul Smith, Penhaligon's, Rachel Riley, Rebecca Hossack Gallery, Toni & Guy

Italy
Atelier Aimée, Armani, Buccellati, Bottega Veneta, Cesare Paciotti, Costume National, Davide Cenci, Dolce & Gabbana, Etro, Fendi Casa, Gianni Versace, Gucci, Lexington ENT, Luca Luca, MonnaLisa, Muska Milano, Oreste / Borsa Jewelers, Paul & Shark, Piero Guidi, Salvatore Ferragamo, Sermoneta Gloves, Trussardi

Israel
Yigal Azrouël

Japan

A Bathing Ape, Comme des Garçons, Issey Miyake, Kansai Yamamoto, Matsuda, Niwaka, Yohji Yamamoto

Korea
E-Land, Who A.U., Pinky Otto, Uniqlo

Lebanon
Reem Bridal's Inc.

Mexico
Grupo Carso S.A. de C.V.

Netherlands
Oilily de Hollande

Portugal
The Best Chocolate Cake

Spain
Carrera y Carrera, Loewe, Lladró, Tous, Zara

Sweden
Dunderdon

Switzerland
Chatila, DeLaneau, Fogal, Kwiat, Toy Watch

United States
Aaron Basha, Auffrance, Babel Fair, Barneys Co-Op, Bill Blass, Bond
No. 9, Brooks Brothers, Coach, Dahesh Museum, DDC Lab, Donna

Karan, Dusica Dusica, Etienne Aigner, Financier Patisserie, Flora and Henri, Florsheim, Fresh, Giggle, Guess, Iris Boutique, Leggiadro, L.O.L. Kids, Judith Leiber, Mallet, Michael Kors, Miguelina, Morrel, Morton's Steakhouse, Ralph Lauren, Reem Acra, Robert Marc Opticians, Round About, Searle, Tui Lifestyle

Disclaimer

This memoir reflects my personal experiences, impressions, and opinions. Some details and events are based on my best recollection and perspective. Nothing in this book is intended to harm or defame any individual, living or deceased, but simply to describe — to the best of my ability — the narrative of what happened in my life, good, bad and indifferent...

www.ingramcontent.com/pod-product-compliance
Lightning Source LLC
Chambersburg PA
CBHW070603130626

46556CB00001B/260